Teach Because I Came!

By Michele Owes

Teach Because I Came!

Editors:

Dr. Diana P. Cherry
Dr. Amenta Crouch
Rhonda K. LaGarde

Dedication

This book is dedicated to my children from whom I have learned tremendously. This book is also written on behalf of God's children who must overcome seemingly insurmountable obstacles to realize their dreams and appreciate their own abilities. We see you. We care for you and we are learning how to better serve you.

With Purposed Hope

Teach Because I Came!

Table of Contents

Foreword   8

Introduction   10

Acknowledgements   12

An Unplanned Journey   14

The Agreement   22

Environmental Setting   27

Who Will Occupy the Smart Classroom?   30

Teach Because I Came   33

A Unique Perspective   49

Generation Z   50

Generation Z - Statistically Speaking   57

Experiences with Generation Z   79

     Trina Z   81

     The Curser   88

     The Sharers   96

     The Network   98

     Calculating the Loss   102

     Baby Doll Z– Present But Not Really   105

     Sexuality and Generation Z   109

There are Consequences 117

The Great Divide: The Educator &the Student 120

Share-worthy Experiences with Educators 123

Economics Class 124

The Caring Teacher 129

Making New History – Working Together 132

Order! Order in the Court! 137

My First Visit to the Principal's Office 139

The English Teacher 143

Call to Personal Duty

A Message to All Students – Know Your Role 145

Education – A Broader Scope 155

A Comprehensive Educational Plan 156

The NAPP (Nutrition, Academics,

Physical & Psychosocial) Program

Nutrition 161

Academics 169

Know Your Audience 171

Identify Your Resources 177

Multiple Intelligences – Simply Put 179

What You Bring to the Learning Exp. 187

Teach Because I Came!

Table in the Back & the Teacher's Aide   191

Summer School   195

Designated Subject Groups (DSG)   196

Classroom Monitors   199

Physical Education   200

Psychosocial Services   203

Alternative Therapies   205

Parental Involvement   206

Confirmation of Purpose   210

The Call to Unity   214

Irony and the School Board Meeting   219

With Great Purpose Comes   230
   Great Responsibility

Works Consulted   231

Foreword

At the forefront of every task is the reason for which one feels driven or purposed. Somewhere in the midst of the assignment you learn that God, a multi-tasker by nature, is always working to accomplish more than you can imagine through your obedience. Your willingness to be a vessel, not out of who you are, but by submitting to who He needs you to be at a given moment, can produce extraordinary results. On this journey as a parent shadowing a male student in high school, I would soon learn that the purpose for my presence had less to do with my child than originally believed. He was simply a catalyst.

There were many things that I silently witnessed that tugged at my heart. Many moments were spent in prayer on behalf of the teachers, the students and for me. I enjoyed the triumphant classroom episodes experienced when the desire to learn met the desire to teach. I left unfulfilled when opportunities to teach were missed due to administrative requirements or when opportunities to learn were thwarted by pride and perceived peer judgment. Nonetheless, I hereby determine that education should be fun and is at its best during interactive learning. During this once-in-a-lifetime experience, I prayed that God would give me understanding, opportunity, and the right words. He responded mightily on all fronts. In some areas I witnessed His handiwork immediately. In other areas I am assured that it is already done. Those things yet to come will rest on the tables of your hearts as the content of this manuscript calls us to action on behalf of our children.

At the end of my tenure as a 51 year old high school student, I felt privileged to experience all that had befallen me. I was honored to be an eye witness to this momentary snapshot in time. I was humbled to know that for this, I was chosen.

For HIS Purpose,

Introduction

As an educator, an involved parent, and first generation student of integration, education and all of its nuances are deeply embedded in the chambers of my heart. Education is unquestionably the most underrated inalienable right. Critical to the quality of life and liberty and necessary for the furtherance of progress is the education of our citizens. At the crux of every crime, whether white collar or blue collar, is the lack of, or misuse of an education. Alternatively, at the root of every good and successful deed is the proper application of an education. Mankind must have knowledge and properly apply it to the issues of life if he is to ever know his inherent greatness!

It is our goal, after sharing eye-witness experiences, to provide more than an opinion, but concrete answers and viable solutions to this educational dilemma of the 21st century. Education is a major component of our nation's success; therefore, there is no room for failure or lackadaisical response. It requires urgent attention, utmost commitment and swift action to solve this crisis.

Citizen-focused nations deem the education of its people as a high-level priority; ranking not less than but equal to national security. Educated minds can and will develop goods and services necessary to prosper a nation. Should the phrase, "the greater the investment, the greater the reward" be coupled with the education of our citizens, rather than the stock market, we could realize a greater America.

Every life has great purpose. Education better prepares each individual to fulfill purpose and to make their contribution to a greater good. Purpose is not given for man to determine, it is entrusted to him to fulfill. If each student, parent and educator approached education from the vantage point of purpose, much more would be achieved. It is from the perspective of *purposed hope* that this manuscript is shared.

For the LORD of hosts hath purposed, and who shall disannul it? and his hand is stretched out, and who shall turn it back?   *Isaiah 14:27*

Acknowledgements

It is because of God's commitment to mankind, through Jesus Christ, that such a book could be written. I am humbled to be a vessel and the pen of a ready writer. Thank you for the clarity of expression and the certainty of your instructions. May all that you desire manifest for the good of your children.

Thank you to my incredible family: my husband (who believes in me and encourages my best), my children (our contribution to mankind), those who were responsible for raising me; my parents (Mom you are the best and Dad who rests in eternal glory), siblings and extended family. I *must* thank my church, From the Heart Church Ministries® whose commitment to God's vision for the local church labored to teach me, mature me and position me for such a task. For every sacrifice, encouragement, chastisement and investment, I earnestly thank you. Because of God's grace, our difficulties have strengthened us, our challenges have matured us and our joys helped stabilize us. I love you.

I am grateful for every student that I met, observed, served and encouraged. Thank you for renewing my mind. My appreciation for everyone who encouraged me and graciously agreed to be a part of this project is immeasurable. You know who you are. You answered the call of necessity and I am grateful to God for you.

And the Lord answered me, and said, write the vision,
and make it plain upon tables, that he may run
that readeth it.   *Habakkuk 2:2*

An Unplanned Journey

In an unexpected and unplanned turn of events, as a 51 year old female, I returned to high school. The reasons were not as glamorous as background preparation for a Hollywood movie or a famous documentary. In hindsight, I understand that it was for a purpose undetermined by me. After receiving a progress report card and being slightly confused by some of the comments and hearing a moving open invitation extended by the counselors on Parents Night, I determined that I would spend my day off at the local high school. My journey was not to find fault but to find solutions to aid success and provide further instructions in the life of a teenager.

Everything I knew about education was being overhauled through the account of my teenager. Statements such as, "Mom, we don't take notes anymore because they don't give us notes. We get a copy of a *Power Point* presentation when it is time to study." Could this be true, I questioned? Why does the school supply list request notebooks if they don't plan for students to use the paper? Most importantly, have they forgotten the direct correlation between writing notes in one's own handwriting and the ability to recall? Are they aware that recall is increased when students read and review what they have written? Is note taking now considered passé?

More shocking was, "Mom, we don't have to bring in a printed copy of our reports or papers. We send it by email only." Really, I questioned? Is paper being replaced by emailed assignments? Surely we could save a tropical rain forest by ceasing paper productions; however, email is not always reliable. There are times when networks fail, emails show up much later than when sent and sometimes they indicate they are sent and the participant never receives them. These occurrences increase or decrease depending on the carrier. Why take the chance of relying on technology when responsibility could be taught by requesting a printed copy?

I had so many questions that I believed deserved answers. I wondered why my child's lunch came back home with him every day, still in the backpack. He was a football player. He needed energy to perform his duties both on and off the field. We always provided a nutritious, home cooked breakfast before school and he packed his own lunch. Was it enough food to carry him throughout the day? I thought not. We tried paying for hot lunch for a few days. When he ate the fast food, he had stomach distress. So he went back to packing his lunch nightly but it kept coming back home. I did not want him to faint on the field. How was he eating? I decided that firsthand knowledge might be the best answer so off to high school I went.

One might only submit to such reordering of a mature life when a few pre-existing conditions exists. You must first be willing to respect individual and collective purpose so greatly that you fear hindering it by your own inaction. Some might call it love. Some may view it as overly involved. However, I simply see it as a manifestation of *hope for the future*. My hope moved me to action. I had a perceived purpose or emphatic reason for going, but in the end, I learned that there was a greater plan for the time period than I imagined.

I have great respect and appreciation for the educational system that nurtured me. All of its working parts: principals, teachers, counselors, administrative staff, coaches, custodial staff, librarians, etc., fulfilled their assigned duties in my life. I found that to be true even today. It was their commitment to education that permitted me to accompany a young man on his daily grind in high school for an undisclosed period of time.

I call it a daily grind because returning to high school helped me to understand it is really for the young mind, young body and the young heart. The organization of a typical day had youthfulness at the center of all planning. The changing of classes and teachers every 45-50 minutes, along with different teaching styles, different classrooms, different classmates, different assignments, etc; all accomplished in a seven hour day was interesting and mentally exhausting for my previously perceived razor-sharp mind. Before the journey was over, I questioned the sharpness of the razor and the fitness of my mind. Nonetheless, it was an experience that reshaped my view of high school and my responsibility as a parent during this season of my child's life.

Teach Because I Came!

Parents were welcomed to participate in many ways at this public high school. In fact, they so desired our help that they scheduled education classes for parents as well. Parents were invited for coffee with the principal and were allowed to have input and exchange ideas. Our absenteeism was so apparent that a four page document was developed outlining all the ways that parents could become involved with the school system. Classroom visits was just one of many options that could be chosen.

Parent visits had to be scheduled and announced to the teachers. With the counselors help, I set up ongoing appointments. I confirmed my presence, at a minimum once a week. If my appointments were overshadowed by state testing or scheduled exams, I swapped my visits to another day. I wanted to see education at work rather than education planned because the parents were coming. My goal after the first several weeks became to confirm my arrival so close to the hour that some might miss the notification.

Eventually I phoned the counselor and asked that she inform the teachers that my off day could conceivably be Monday, Thursday or Friday. These days could be altered by my work load; however, I would certainly be there each week, though I might not confirm which day. She forwarded the email and thanked me for being an *involved parent*. Something about that term *involved parent*, stuck in my mind.

I did not question my role as a parent. I accepted it wholeheartedly but, was I really *involved*? I checked assignment books, looked on the Parent-Info Line to check grades and read teacher comments. I reacted to whatever was posted good or bad? Was that *involved*?

In that instant, I realized that I had bought into the theory that high school students required less parental involvement. As a result of my visits, I wholeheartedly believe the opposite. High school is one of the most vulnerable times in a child's life. They are too old to do what they used to do (elementary type things) and too young to do what they want to do (be independent, make all their own rules, make their own choices about everything). It is the *misfit* period of life. Pedophiles and child molesters have mastered the uncertainty of this period of development and capitalized on it by becoming friends and confidants. Yet as parents, the thought tends to be offer more independence because they are getting older, when less is the better option.

According to the Center for Disease Control and Prevention, suicide is rising among teens. In 2009, suicide for individuals between the ages of 15-24, was 10.1%.[1] It is the highest rate recorded in sixteen years. The National Institute for Drug Abuse reports its highest rise in daily marijuana use amongst 8th, 10th and 12th graders in 2010. After marijuana, prescription drugs were most frequently used.[2] Alcohol use among 12th graders was at

---

[1] American Foundation for Suicide Prevention, 2010, <http://www.afsp.org/index.cfm?page_id=04ea1254-bd31-1fa3-c549d77e6ca6aa37> (accessed April 2012).

[2] National Institute for Drug Abuse, "Statistics and Trends," April 2012, <http://www.drugabuse.gov/drugs-abuse/alcohol> (accessed June 2012).

43.7%. With statistics such as these, why do we leave our students alone?

Parenting styles are supposed to adjust to this new evolving person, soon to be an adult. Granted experiences that build trust and self confidence are to be an ongoing part of the relationship, but where does high school fit in? What exactly is the role of a parent during high school years, not only to our child, but to the school system in which they are a part? Is the tax dollar our only contribution?

My Mom volunteered as the school nurse at my elementary school once a month. She took a day off work each month to serve. We had a school nurse but in her absence, parents volunteered. Mom walked two miles to get there and walked home with me. Was I that committed or involved? I would say not.

I responded to every call made from the school. I attended every meeting of which I was aware. The school used a phone dialing system that notified parents of scheduled events. I really appreciated that because my student was more interested in his own assignments and duties than informing me of meetings designed for the parents.

I checked grades regularly and contacted teachers as needed. I thanked every teacher each year and made the following statement. "If my child ever demonstrates anything less than the utmost respect for you and your class, call me, or his father, on the first day. Please do not allow it to happen more than once. You have the responsibility to teach, we have the responsibility to parent. We are here to help you as you help our child progress in his education. We work together and I will support you any way that I can. This not only includes behavior but assignments. If he misses one, please call us on the first day."

Teachers seemed to appreciate the support and occasionally we received a phone call. Our response was swift and we followed up to confirm the desired change. If the progress report showed signs of difficulty, I made the phone call to find out where the issues were and how they could be improved. I requested input from both the teacher and the student. However, I responded within my role as a parent. My child also had to accept responsibility for his own progress by contacting the teacher to find out what had to be done to improve his/her standing in the class and perform as required.

The real lesson learned during these weeks of high school boot camp was not about teachers or schools, it was about the children. As I share these experiences, it is my hope as parents, educators and students that we hear the heartbeat and the heart's cry from our children.

Some might argue that a random sample should be required for the contents of this writing to be held true. Notwithstanding, I found the eye witness experience with our children's daily routines invaluable and greater than experimental conjecture.

The Agreement

Considering the impact that my return to high school might have on my son, we took the time to reach an agreement. He was a visible student athlete who was reasonably popular. He also happened to be quite charismatic having never met a stranger. With that said, he was also adjusting to a new state, a new school and a new found popularity. Arguably, my presence on the campus could upset the delicate balance that he had worked to achieve.

Our older children thought it was high school suicide to have your parent on campus. They strongly advised against it. Frankly, they could not understand why parent teacher conferences were not sufficient enough as they had been for them. I could not actually explain the unction but it was significant enough for me to respect their opinion but not follow it. My husband reminded me that parenting was an adult responsibility. He smiled and said most children would not agree; however, if I felt led to do so, he encouraged me to move forward. Consequently, I spoke to my high school student and we established some ground rules for my visits.

I offered to make my visits as anonymous as possible. It was necessary to let him know my purpose was not to embarrass him or humiliate him. Ultimately, I was returning to high school to be a help. To what extent I did not know. I shared my plan to sit in the back of the room and observe. I promised not to walk with him or try to talk to him until he came home from school. I could be a teacher monitor or class visitor, just not an embarrassing parent. Ultimately, I did not care what anyone thought. The need to ensure that my son would matriculate through the educational process was greater than my thought for his feelings or anyone else's. For sanity sake, if anyone asked who I was, I was prepared to say that I was an observer because that was the truth. Nobody needed to know who I was and I would confidently protect that knowledge.

The school counselor was instrumental in helping me keep my promise. She asked the teachers not to introduce me or state who I was but to allow me to quietly observe. They agreed and conducted their classes accordingly.

Instantly the unexpected began to happen. First, every student was curious as to who I was and why I was there. I was an enigma. It seemed that they had not seen an adult in their classrooms observing before. Apparently, I was the first per the student's chatter. This was surprising because they were seniors. Secondly, my son would not deny me. He publicly owned me. As other students played the guessing game, he spoke up with great authority.

"She's my mom," he said admirably. I sat in astonishment. He broke the code of anonymity. I was prepared to keep it for the duration of the school year or until the end of the burden to make this pilgrimage to high school. He could not last one day. While I was stunned, I was also proud of him. I shudder to think how I might have felt if he had denied me. Maybe I would have felt like Jesus when His disciples denied him. Although in this case there was no thirty pieces of silver.

Several students echoed, "Jay is in trouble."

"No I'm not," he reported. "She really wants to see how my day goes."

Unsolicited, a female commented, "Jay you have a great mom. I wish my mom would come to school with me and see how my day goes. She used to when I was in Jr. High. I loved it when she came."

One by one the comments poured in, "Yeah, all parents should come at least once. Then I think our teachers would teach more or teach better. I wish my parents would come. Then they would understand why I say I don't get this Algebra II," another shared.

With my presence positively confirmed by youngsters thirty plus years my junior, I felt purpose was being fulfilled. Though this generation was certainly not my peer, and I did not personally perceive peer pressure, their disapproval could have presented unforeseen difficulties both at school and at home. It was good to be widely accepted, even as a parent. The teacher himself was so surprised by the comments he gave me a smile and a nod.

Unlike popular belief, students openly admitted that they wanted their parents to come to high school at least once. Even the teacher was surprised by their response. A parent on campus was not high school suicide after all.

Rather, it was a high-five time. I was actually appreciated. We had all breached the fear of the unknown and found it poignantly pleasant.

By week three I was socially accepted in all classes. Students stopped staring and started smiling. I smiled too. The typical greeting was "Hi Jay's Mom." I responded with genuine respect and joy. I truly enjoyed my time with the young people. I made a point to speak to and smile at everyone. I understood that high school could be tough and I certainly did not want to be a negative influence.

Interestingly enough, the coaches were concerned as to why I was on the campus. They questioned my son and asked if he was in trouble. He gave them the same response that he gave in class, which was true. It was then that he learned that schools expected to see parents at the games, at booster club meetings, at parent-teacher meetings and at graduation. They were alarmed to see us on campus at any other time. They did an extra grade check to make sure he was eligible. The athletic director questioned my presence as well.

The coach's wife taught one of the classes and personally asked why I was there. I gave her the same response as the others. My son thought it was funny that my presence caused the athletic department to ask so many questions. He reassured them that all was well.

I found it interesting that the students seemed to really appreciate my presence and wanted me in their classrooms. However, some teachers, coaches and principals seemed to be on high-alert because of my presence. They found it hard to believe that a parent cared enough to spend their day off in a high school classroom, especially since I was not part of the booster club.

It is critical to note that my mission was not fully disclosed even to me. I simply had a strong burden/unction to go to the high school. I love teachers and enjoyed seven years of being one. I fully support the educational process, particularly education based on inclusion.

Students learn differently and the value of their education is only as good as their inclusion in the educational process, understanding that their different learning styles are not ignorance or inability, just difference. My visitations afforded me the opportunity to understand the environment and see possibilities to supplement the learning process at home.

Environmental Setting

The public high school referenced is located in the Southwestern Region of the United States. It has a population of over 2500 students, mixed with upper, middle and low income students. I encountered approximately 180 students per day with the changing of classes. College prep, basic and state testing classes were attended lending to a wide range of student populations.

One could not have selected a more beautiful atmosphere with the backdrop of the mountains on every side. Sunshine was the predominant weather forecast 95% of the time. The occasional earth tremor, known as the earthquake and strong winds (20-60 mph) were more common than anything else as atmospheric conditions. The school was positioned in a community of new homeowners, fairly affluent, with properties less than seven years old. However, the school zoning included much of the lower income populace within seven miles of its location yielding to a blend of social and economic classes.

The school buildings and developed surrounding property were less than five years old. Substandard, damaged, or dilapidated conditions were not contributors to student performance or outlook. The architectural design was multiple separate two-story buildings, adjacent one to another, creating courtyards and plenty of open spaces.

The high school is state of the art. Every classroom is considered *smart* containing electronic boards and built in projectors. English classes were scheduled next to the technology lab which to my surprise was loaded with laptops. If one failed to work, it was simply swapped out for another. Students were assigned their own laptop during classes and the "flash drive on a neck chain" ruled the day. Banished were the days of *I left my paper at home.*

Security policed the grounds regularly to make sure students were in their designated places, or had a pass to detour from the prescribed direction. The restrooms were locked and the teacher's key was required for entry. Security patrolled the restrooms immediately after the bell rang to ensure students were not hiding or using them as havens to ditch classes.

Security was strategically assigned around the campus with walkie-talkies, to have a birds-eye view and communicate about any movement after the bell rang. They also rode bicycles to make their rounds. The environment was clean, organized and secure.

Course offerings catered to every level of learning including honors classes, college prep classes, basic education and skills classes such as automotive and culinary. The educators considered their entire student body and provided the necessary educational opportunities for success. By all appearances, it was a great school and well prepared for its students.

Books were in each classroom having enough for each student on the roster. An extra set of books was sent home with each student at the beginning of the semester to ensure that students had the tools to study at home. Gone was the responsibility of remembering which books to take home or to school on which days.

The administrative staff was supportive, respectful and excited about their jobs. Teachers, counselors, principals, etc. were degreed and accredited. The state had determined the pace at which students would be taught via objectives and incentives. The plans were made and any hindrance to education, within their control, was removed.

With all of the foresight and meticulous planning by educators, coupled with the right and authority to educate our children, the school's test scores seemingly should have been spectacular. As with any school district, the one component that cannot be planned, yet is the most critical to its success, is the student. Who will occupy the smart classroom?

Who Will Occupy the *Smart* Classroom?

With such outstanding preparation beforehand, the missing ingredient and wild card (incalculable impact) in the formula for education was and always will be *the student*. Who will occupy the seats of the *smart classroom*? *Who*, remaining both nameless and faceless, will be a part of this learning experience? Who will dine on the educational feast that the educators have prepared? Will they be able to digest the intake and make it strength for their journey?

Who (meaning person) will complement the level of preparation and planning of the *smart classroom*? What will be the temperament, personality, moral fiber and educational acumen of the students who occupy the seats? What type of behavior, demeanor and manner will manifest in this well planned classroom? What emotional, hormonal, or social difficulties will arise during the school year? Will traumatic events occur in the life of a student during the school year? How will these factors affect the student's willingness to participate in the learning process? Will the student be able to cope with the issues of their lives and focus on their education?

Who will occupy the smart classroom? Will they have an expectation for learning? Will their expectations be met? What social dynamics will develop among this group? Will the peer pressure to be thin, popular, or sexually active overwhelm the student populace or will they maintain a healthy personal identity? In the midst of all the social issues will students remain dedicated and loyal to their own education?

The responses to each question present an undetermined factor able to undermine or undergird the educational process. These are the *"wildcards"* that can thwart the success of even the best planned educational institutions. These are also the factors that most educational institutions that accredit and train educators, administrators and counselors, do not address.

Is it possible to make learning so exciting that the student will forget about who they are, or are not, long enough to learn? How does a teacher successfully navigate through the *wildcards* without losing control and missing the valuable opportunities to teach and provoke learning? How does a teacher teach the seemingly unreachable/ unteachable student? How does a teacher maintain control in the classroom while nurturing an atmosphere of freedom of discovery and welcoming of new ideas? The real answers to the aforementioned questions are rooted far away from the classroom; however, they greatly affect what happens in it.

Who prepares our educators for the unknowns? Whose responsibility is it to teach educators how to successfully navigate through the maze and capitalize on the opportunity to teach? Where does one receive such training?

The inability to navigate and positively address the *wildcards* in education represents *the little foxes that spoil the vine*. While educators are professionally trained to teach, one must also complement their training with measures to overcome hindrances to the main objective – teaching.

The following story embodies the challenges that can occur in the smart classroom. As an eye witness, I experienced behaviors, attitudes and actions that from the initial onset appeared to be rude and expulsion worthy. After battling the personal desire to judge, through prayer and closer observation, what I perceived as obnoxious behavior was revealed as the cries of our children longing to be participants in the educational process.

Students desire more than to be planned for: they desire *to participate in* the education process. They bring a wealth of knowledge, experience and abilities to the learning environment and they simply desire the opportunity to share and to participate. They desire to do more than receive what has been planned. Their greater desire is to contribute to the process, not only for themselves but for others. When the opportunity does not exist to participate, they will labor together to create one that distracts rather than complement the learning process. Take this journey with me as a fifty-one year old high school student.

Teach Because I Came!

It was during the 7:30AM Algebra class that a young man who sat one table away from my seat in the back, unconsciously became a hindrance to the learning process. The word *unconsciously* seems to best describe the ease with which he espoused profanity in between sentences. It was clear that he saw no problem cursing in the presence of adults (the teacher and me). Though my eyes met his each time he used bad language, he refrained not. After the first fifteen minutes I recognized that the teacher did not take occasion to harness the distasteful behavior nor seemed to be taken aback by it.

In addition to this student's improper word choices was a need to chatter constantly about his inability to understand the subject matter -Algebra II. Mutterings such as, "I don't get this! I don't understand! This does not make any sense," along with expletives. Then there was one question that caused me to perk up. *"When did you teach us this? I don't remember you teaching this."*

The teacher continued to write without responding and completed the examples on the board. There was no question in my mind that he knew the material and was quite knowledgeable in this area of instruction. He whizzed through the examples as one with great command, comfort and understanding of Algebra II. I considered myself a copious note taker with years of experience, but I could not keep up with him. He was, in my mind, *an Einstein*. The Bachelors degree, previous work on a Master's program and Neurofeedback certification did not help me. I could not keep up. I had begun to feel like my comrade the Curser, *left behind.*

I really wanted to copy everything off the board and write down the extra comments he made. My hope was to review it later at home with my student. Sadly, I failed. I could not get it all. In fact, I missed much of the work trying not to be a distraction while in the class. Before I knew it, I had the same sentiment as the student seated at the table before me. I did not understand.

I loved Algebra in high school. Why was it so foreign to me today? I enjoyed mathematics of all kind until I got to statistics (which I passed by the grace of God) in college. What happened to me today? Was I influenced by the negativity before me or was the speed at which the lesson was instructed too fast for this "old mind"? Like the Curser, I wondered, had I been taught this before?

The question had the potential to open Pandora's Box and eventually it did. As the teacher was going over homework problems on the white board with the class, the student was inquiring whether prior instruction had been given. In essence, there was a bold insinuation that the students were assigned homework from lessons where no previous instruction had taken place. In short, students were to teach themselves through homework and self discovery. The teacher's answer told the story.

Unwilling to be ignored, the Curser repeated the same mutterings. "I don't get this! I don't understand! This does not make any sense!" Present also were the nonverbal communication cues such as rubbing the face, constantly readjusting of the posture, tapping the pencil, and sighing loudly. One cannot leave out the expletives he used. There was that question *again* that caused me to perk up. *"When did you teach us this? I don't remember you teaching this."*

The teacher responded very calmly. This entire class should have learned these principles and algorithms in Algebra I. He went on to say that those were basic and elementary steps in Algebra I and if they had not learned them, they should not be in his class. I gasped internally.

What a snare? From that moment all questions and murmuring around the classroom ceased. The courage to ask for and gain knowledge was knowingly choked from those who lacked understanding. The burden for obtaining knowledge was shifted to the previous year, previous teacher, or even to the students because they did not remember. More questions would have been an open admission that they did not belong in Algebra II, should not have passed Algebra I, and made them subject to belittling responses.

I looked around the room to see who might have the courage to challenge this standoff with the earnest desire to learn despite what might have been forgotten. There was none. Heads were up on the question of when the material was taught. All heads were down as students tried to teach themselves what they did not understand.

I began to feel uncomfortable. I sensed the joy that I had about coming to school ebbing away from me. I had a long day ahead of me and so I silently prayed that God would grant me understanding of the material and help me not to be distracted or disturbed by anyone or anything. I wanted to learn what He desired to teach me while I was there. I asked if I could in some way be a vessel for His glory on these school grounds and to these children. I certainly wanted to be a help to my own child so I silently prayed for the teacher, students and myself.

Internally, I was angered by the disrespectful response from the teacher. Albeit, the Cursers actions were less than appreciative, I found the teachers remarks offensive. I failed to see how it could motivate learning. In an effort to protect his integrity, the teacher created a stumbling block to learning. The block was so big that even I was having difficulty getting over it.

At the moment my prayer ended, understanding was granted. Not as I had hoped, in terms of Algebraic calculations, but in terms of the people who sat before me. The moment I sought understanding was the moment my perspective was significantly changed.

As obnoxious as the cursing and constant chatter had become to me as the visitor in the back, in a moment my understanding was enlightened. By some divine revelation, I understood him. His chatter and cursing was his cry for help. He had a need to understand the material and the speed at which it was taught was like running alongside a racecar on the Indianapolis Speedway. His chatter was his way of saying, slow this car down. I need to catch up. Will anyone allow me to get on board?

With new understanding, I began to admire his tenacity. Silenced for a moment to ponder whether he belonged in Algebra II, his verbal assault was reenergized. Underneath everything that was inappropriate was a confidence that someone was responsible for teaching him and he would talk and curse until they came to his rescue.

This young student was not asking to be held captive to last year's lesson plans or the effectiveness of the teacher he had before, nor did he want to be charged for what his brain did not recall. He was there and now was the moment for learning because he wanted to learn. This was the moment for instruction because he perceived there were tools missing from his tool box that were necessary to be successful in Algebra II. Though rudely, he pursued knowledge the way he knew how.

Critics might say that students should not drive or steer the course of instruction. If not the student, then who steers? Who can best determine if there is a gap in their knowledge? Waiting for test or quiz results to measure outcome is waiting too long when the overt signs are present.

Teachers often say they want students who desire to learn. They want to teach those who want to be educated. The first rule of education is to know your audience. The student is the audience. When the audience is screaming, "I do not understand," it warrants a repeat of the lesson, a reiteration of concepts, or even a reassuring commitment to visit the student's table at the earliest moment possible.

My train of thought as an educator began to race. It was difficult to corral back into the current classroom experience. I wondered if modern teacher training includes instructions geared to recognizing when students required more instruction. Are teachers trained not to judge the value of their lesson plan by whether they completed it, or rather by answering the question, "Did learning take place today? Did the light bulbs turn on for my students today?" Moreover, are teachers tasked to review and or re-teach concepts that students may not recall? If not, who has this responsibility in our educational system? As I refocused on the classroom, I asked myself, could five minutes of review have saved this lesson plan? Could this have been an opportunity to provoke learning and encourage the heart of these students? Will this opportunity come again?

Self condemnation quickly set in. How could I have so quickly, and so judgmentally, misidentified the needs of this student? My perceived purpose for being there was to help one student, but my horizon was broadened, my coast was enlarged. There was a greater need before me. My perceived purpose was simply a catalyst. By understanding the Curser, I understood the frustrations of my own child. By experiencing the class I learned how maddening it is to watch a lesson end and your own understanding has not begun! It was revealed that the Curser and his classmates were attempting to do homework without understanding the material.

Fighting back the river inside, I realized that this student had a need and the system under which he was assigned was unable to recognize it. He was much more than an obnoxious student with bad language habits. He was a young man trying to be a participant in the learning process. He wanted to be a successful contributor. After being shut down by pride and arrogance, he was able to rise above the bold insult and press for what he needed.

Most of the students in his class remained silent for a while in fear of their own reputation, not only in the eyes of the teacher but fellow students as well. Who can bear being perceived as slow, dumb, stupid or as one who was socially promoted rather than academically deserving?

The Curser's frustration and verbal outbursts eventually led to a mutiny at his table. Soon every student at his table began to voice their frustration and inability to understand the subject matter. Their table was not the only one. It caught on like a wild fire.

A male student turned around to me, the unidentified visitor sitting in the back of the classroom, and asked, "Do you understand this?" I froze. I did not want to feed into the frenzy of revolt. While taking personal inventory, I smiled. My private internal conversation went like this...I am an adult. I respect and appreciate all teachers. For God's sake I *was* one. I will not say or do anything to undermine the authority in this classroom. Nor will I do anything to have my privilege revoked as an observer in this class. As much as I wanted to respond, I held my peace. I smiled even the more.

Understanding the war in my mind, he politely changed the question to, "Did you take Algebra before?" Thank God! I was okay to answer this one. "Yes, I did," I responded.

"How did you do?" he continued.

Proudly I reported, "I made A's".

"Then you understand this and you can help me, yes?" He uttered and smiled back knowing he had set me up.

When he finished the question, three other students from his table turned around awaiting my answer. They were hoping I could be the teacher's aide that was so desperately missing in that class. Amazed at how he masterfully backed me into a corner, I smiled at each of them.

I would not mislead them. Instead I had to admit my own weakness. Reluctantly I confessed, "I made A's, but I do not understand this. I am sorry. Let's keep trying. We will get it." Disappointed by my answer, they all turned back around in unison.

A young lady at the same table seemed to sense the self disappointment. She turned to me and politely said, "It is okay. Only one person in this class really understands what is going on. He is the guy at the table over there in the blue hoodie. He just seems to get it. He might know more than the teacher. The rest of us, we just keep trying."

I smiled and responded, "Don't ever stop trying."

"I won't," she confirmed.

A chilling thought crossed my mind. Are our students so desperate for education that they will request it of a complete stranger, while their teacher is present? Do I have the look, demeanor or sign on my face that reads: *Willing to help all students! I believe in you.* Should I have been flattered that they instantly trusted that I could help or was I to be suspect of their lack of respect for the teacher in the classroom?

This cry of desperation reached four tables in the room including the one directly in front of me? Did the students realize that one teacher is unable to reach them all? Did they expect me to come to their table and begin to teach? What was happening here? What does this really mean? One thing was clear - I had more questions than answers.

As an educator who had long before moved to another career, it never entered my mind that these students were not my responsibility. Nor did I believe that it was acceptable to ignore a cry for help. I was deeply saddened that my brain could not comprehend or keep up with the race car speed instruction that began at the drop of the checkered flag, known as the bell.

Had I been able to understand, I would have continued to volunteer on my day off to be the help that the students needed. In lieu of being an observer, I would have become the unpaid teacher's aide. Unable to comprehend, I left feeling quite inadequate.

Feelings of inadequacy rarely crept into my personal life, certainly none as strong as the ones experienced on that day. Yet, this was the feeling of 99% of this class as they exited the room on most days. I had experienced some success and had a few accomplishments; I would overcome such a heavy weight. What did these students have? Their lives were just beginning. Did they even know how to refocus?

My hope was to come to school to refresh and learn what was necessary to help my child, who was not having much success in this particular class. Per his counselor, he had more credits than necessary to graduate (as a result of a state transfer) and go on to college. However, most four year colleges required successful completion of Algebra II for acceptance. In short, Algebra II was critical to every student in the class.

There was a barrier to education present in the classroom. Having no foreknowledge of the cause, the certainty is that it occurred before my time of observance. Whether causality was due to previous grade levels, previous Algebra classes, a student's home life, themselves, or their teachers, it was present that day.

This experience left me with an inescapable burden. It would not be dismissed. It prompted me to extend my time of visitation. In fact, I was burdened to do more than simply talk about education, but to be a help. The burden is still carried in the backpack of my heart. It was ever present throughout my time on the high school campus.

My perspective and depth of perception changed as I departed Algebra II that morning. I was given the rare opportunity to walk in the student's shoes. This was a poignant and rare occasion for me. It is one that I both cherished and disdained. Clearly this experience helped me to understand the utterances of my child. More purposed was the heartfelt experience of being the student who did not understand. It was the first time in my life that I tried to apply myself academically and failed miserably.

I will resist the urge to mention the number of times I picked up the Algebra II book when my son had a question and after repeated review was unable to answer. Returning to school was to help overcome the silence of inadequacy that I felt when I was unable to help. I had written curriculum for schools and yet I did not understand Algebra II, even after attending class.

Would that I could return to work and politely forget this experience. The innocent faces that turned to a total stranger sitting in the back (me) for help are faces not easily erased. The depth of their disappointment was unexpected and painful. I did not know their names, nor did they know mine, but we shared a moment, our paths crossed. It was certainly for a purpose greater than I could perceive. The burden resulted from having an opportunity to help students, something I personally enjoy; however, I was unable to provide what was needed, not unwilling, but unable.

The more the Curser talked, the more I understood. He wanted to graduate and had stated so in his disgruntled dissertation. He was a senior and this class, in his mind, was the key to his future success. He needed this class to go on to college. After the teacher completed his whirlwind examples on the board, he answered a few questions and retreated to his desk for the students to begin seatwork. He gave them a few minutes at the task before rising due to repeated statements like "I don't understand this, I can't do this. Will you help me?" The continued chatter drove the teacher back to the board.

Yeah! Their persistence paid off. Two things came to mind right away. The students were not taking notes from the problems on the board. While I was feverishly trying to keep up, they sat back observing. Why? Because he taught them not to take notes while he taught but to observe. Before the midterm and finals, he gave them typewritten notes that he wanted them to study.

I stared at my student and mouthed the words, *take notes*. He picked up his pencil and began to take notes. The teacher turned around and saw him writing what was on the board. He spoke to him directly and said, "You don't have to take notes. I am going to teach you all this." I will give you the notes I want you to have.

Frozen for a few seconds, my student stopped taking notes and looked at me. I mouthed emphatically, "Take Notes!" Respectfully unwilling to defy his teacher or his parent, he raised his hand and asked the teacher if he could take notes if he wanted to. Reluctantly, the teacher agreed. The students at the table in front of me turned to confirm this as a standard process by saying, "He does not give us many notes in this class." Hearing this, the teacher repeated several times, "I am going to teach you this."

Until that moment, I did not understand how an Algebra student could come home nightly without notes after attending class each day. Here was the answer to why the evening review of notes in class ended so quickly. Herein also was the answer to his difficulty. He was simply relying on his brain to recall what was on a typed study sheet given before test time. Inside I am screaming, "WHO DOES NOT TAKE NOTES IN ALGEBRA? HOW *OLD* AM I?"

Was note taking a dead art in high school? Was it passé? Had it been so long since I was a student, teacher, principal and school administrator that I was out of touch with the methods of today? Had new methodologies mistaken the value of hand-mind coordination and its connection to the brain's ability to recall? If so, it was destroying our homework routine at home.

Our home routine was for each student to spend the first 30-minutes relaxing and unwinding from the day. The next 30 minutes was designated to reading notes taken from each class before beginning homework. The practice of reviewing class notes was to conceptually bring things back to their remembrance and better prepare them to do homework. It also served as a pre-study for tests and quizzes.

I simply could not believe the consistent nightly response that no notes were given in Algebra class. I was wrong and the reality of my lack of understanding of today's classroom was showing up and causing tension at home. What I insisted schools/teachers were doing, they were not. What I practiced and held as the basic laws/methods for education was no longer deemed necessary for success. In short, I owed my child an apology. I simply did not believe that most teachers were not giving notes.

I attributed the emptiness of his notebook to distractions or failure to pay attention in class. I badgered him to get the phone numbers of other students in class to get notes from them prior to tests. I held him totally responsible for missing everything, not once believing that repeatedly notes were not offered. While I worked to manage the emotions from being incredibly wrong, I remember being thankful that this very disbelief is what brought me back to high school.

As I struggled to stop thinking of my need to apologize to my student, I became more conscious of the discussion that took place before me. The teacher said repeatedly, "I am going to teach you this." Then it hit me. These were solutions to the previous night's homework on the board and yet he was saying, "I am going to teach you this. I am going to give you the notes."

The Curser was onto something. His homework required skills that he had not been taught. It is truly possible that the foundation was in last year's lesson plan, but the skills for last night's homework were not taught or instructed in this year's assignments.

Unable to ignore their comments, criticisms and unbridled cry, the teacher began to try to teach an algebra lesson connected to their homework. Then it was clear as he engaged the students, they were able to follow the basic steps along with him. They began to give the answers and tell him the next steps. It was also clear when they reached the area of new information. This is when Mr. Einstein had to teach and not speed through the lesson. I enjoyed a silent cheer for their resilience. They won. He had to teach because they came to learn.

Without the pressure of high school graduation looming over my head, I too came to learn Algebra II. My mind was focused, I had the natural tools necessary to be a part of the learning experience and yet knowledge escaped me.

In a moment of uncharted emotional territory, I began to fight back tears. I am not a highly emotional person or a cry baby as we used to call it. Something about this morning made me feel dumb in spite of all the knowledge I had gained. Through water-filled eyes, I scribbled on my notepad. *Teach, Because I Came.*

Like my younger counterparts, we came ready to learn. We simply needed the educator to *Teach Because We Came.* Not to teach the lesson plan for the day, but to meet us at our level of need and guide us to where we needed to be. This we wanted without being held hostage to last year's lessons, or in my case, 30+ years ago lessons. This we wanted respectfully without condemnation for our lack of knowledge but with encouragement for what we could achieve. On this day, I joined their collective cry, ***Teach Because I Came!***

A Unique Perspective

Many educators, and parents alike, would focus on immediate correction of the Curser's crude language, the outspokenness or even the level of disrespect. Behavior is often addressed first to restore a sense of order and to regain control. While this is a common practice and necessary, it may not be the first order of business. The opportunity to correct such actions would best present itself in a private conversation at the teacher's desk, rather than open rebuke.

When bad behaviors receive the most attention, educators lose the real focus –the opportunity to teach. Rarely are educators taught to examine the cause of the bad behavior. Asking the question, "Why did it show up in my classroom?" can provide some unexpected truths.

Indeed, issues arise outside the classroom that may affect the behavior of students while in the classroom. However, what this algebra teacher witnessed was directly associated with his lesson plan or the lack thereof. Constant sighing with open comments about the lack of understanding was not a personal assault to the teacher but more an admission of need accompanied by an unmet desire to learn. The Curser's method was an unlearned; albeit rude, request to be an active participant in the educational process. Confirmed by their willingness to accept help from a complete stranger, these students were prepared to receive help from anyone who would offer it.

Should educators pause to discover the cause and resist the opportunity to feel embarrassed or upshot, they will find an eager group of learners. *One of the biggest lesson to learn as an educator is that all the planning and preparation is for the good of the student. Education is not about the educator, it simply involves them.*

To his credit, the teacher was clearly knowledgeable; yet, he had not made himself available to meet the needs of the students who were set before him. Few of us can remember all that we learned last year. However, with the correct approach to jog one's memory, we might be willing to try.

When he finally allowed the students to drive the lesson based on their ability to learn and he allowed them to participate he had a different class, one that respected his role and received what he had to offer.

Generation Z

While the educational system of our country has been steadfastly focused on education and our preparation has left no stone unturned in our efforts to prepare for students, our greatest oversight has been the real needs of those whom we are tasked to educate. My journey to high school identifies a specific populace, hereby and henceforth, referred to as *Generation Z*. As the last letter in the alphabet, it is paralleled to our lack of effort to meet this growing need. Generation Z is as much a product of our narrow scope of education as they are a product of horrific economic and life circumstances.

In addition to the typical high school student from a stable two-parent or a single-parent/guardian home is the child whose life experiences have taken them far beyond the world of a high school classroom. The details and issues of their lives rendered the classroom ineffective long before the teacher prepared the lesson plan. For these students, their concerns are deeper than the etchings of chalk on a chalk board, their worries more real than a power-point presentation and their lives more convoluted than most could imagine. These are the students that few teachers reach no matter how well they prepared. Generation Z appears in our smart classrooms and can cause the best of teachers to question their own abilities.

Generation Z dresses for school but the desire for education is not their garment. They are present in body but their minds rarely enter the classroom. Their names are on the roll book but they rarely grant the teacher the opportunity to educate them. These are young, bright minds that *checked out* of high school as one would *check out* a book from the library. On the premises, on the roll, but absent nonetheless. In their present but absent state, there is a cry from the heart, a longing in the eye, a wound so deep that it stops their forward progress. The depth of the occurrence greatly hinders their ability to engage in this critical period of development--their education. These are the students who flood classrooms, frustrate educators, and crowd the educational system with issues that do not conceivably belong to education.

Our educational system is designed to reach every individual at some point in their lives and the primary focus is still simply education. Preparing students to successfully perform on standardized tests is not education; completing the textbook is not education; finishing the lesson plan is not education. These are imposed requirements that can and often have precluded the learning process.

Equipping young people with the necessary tools to function in our society is critical and must become the focus of our educational system. Services that meet their overall needs including secondary issues that involve counseling for abuse, maltreatment and the like must become part of the educational plan. More than preparing the *smart classroom* we must prepare the method by which these students can engage in the education process with successful outcomes.

Generation Z is often a product of incredible loss having suffered atrocities such as child abuse (sexual, physical and mental), child abandonment or child molestation. Children whose parents are incarcerated, those who suffer extreme poverty or homelessness, where alcoholism and drug addiction destroy any semblance of family are encompassed in this new generation of students. Let us not fail to remember those who have survived the torment of domestic violence or experienced extreme neglect. This is only part of the history of Generation Z. Situations beyond their control, not due to their own actions, cloud their lives daily.

As a nation we report the impact of drug trafficking on our borders as a national security event and a tremendous national budget item. Yet we fail to trace the impact of the subsequent drug abuse by parents, guardians, etc., and the effect it has on the children that occupy our classrooms. We report the catastrophes of alcoholism in traffic accidents and fatalities yet overlook the impact alcoholism has on the children raised by alcoholic parents. Nightly news reports the burden of drug addiction and alcoholism on both the legal and health care systems but draws no continuity to the effects on the performance of children in our classrooms. There is an impact as well as a consequence playing as a scripted movie in our classrooms and the characters are in Generation Z.

The rising numbers of the homelessness were highly publicized in relation to their impact on the housing market and the financial system of our country. Strangely, the impact of homelessness on the education of our children has not been aired to the extent of the financial impact. Without question, unstable living conditions affect the lives of our children and can be traced to their overall academic performance.

We report domestic violence as an independent variable paramount to shame and embarrassment. We even create measures to protect women and children yet we miss the opportunity to draw the connection to America's classrooms. The consequences of domestic violence are seated in our classrooms presenting themselves behaviorally, socially and academically. Yet we fail to make the connection strong enough to prepare for their arrival.

Newsworthy is the reporting of billions of dollars spent on child welfare. Having to care for children who have been neglected, abused and malnourished is a tremendous burden on the nation's welfare system. The financial obligation to provide care through foster parents and guardians is immeasurable. There is also an understated toll on our educational system manifesting behaviorally, socially and academically. Yet our educators have not been prepared to meet their needs.

Mental illness, one of the most underfunded health concerns in our country, is not innocent in its impact on our health care system. The lack of proper diagnosis, care and support for family members is astounding. The less than positive effect of such neglect in our health care system breeds consequences that can be traced directly to our classrooms. The results are the same whether students themselves suffer from mental illness or if they are in the care of someone who is mentally ill.

The poor and undocumented individuals living in America impact more than the fiscal budget. Their undocumented status often prevents them from receiving services; therefore, they often live in very poor, uninhabitable conditions. Shelter without basic utilities such as running water, electricity and gas is considered substandard with the possibility of endangerment to a child. For fear of deportation, such students and their families avoid the use of medical, social and other services available in the country to which they flee. Yet, their children manage to occupy a seat in the smart classroom. The impact of poverty and refugee status is a much greater impact on our educational system than simply financial.

The children intricately involved in the outcomes of homelessness, drug and alcohol addiction, mental illness, incarceration and extreme poverty inevitably focus on solutions for their daily concerns rather than on academics. Their concerns are far more basic than the Theory of Relativity. Questions such as will I have a place to live, sleep or eat bombard their thoughts. Worries about parents in prison, on drugs, or threatened by domestic violence conquer their thoughts.

Will anyone be there when I get home? How many days will go by before anyone attends to my needs? These looming questions specific to the basic needs of human beings are common robbers of the focus necessary for good academic performance.

For Generation Z, life holds many uncertainties for which eight hours of education, Monday through Friday, are no match. Academia rarely wins against such distractions unless it offers information and services that meet the needs most often perceived as separate and apart from education. Generation Z is present in our classrooms in greater numbers than one might conceive. They require our utmost attention and help.

The following chapter, *Generation Z – Statistically Speaking,* reveals some astounding facts about the current populace in our school system. As you review the statistics, ask yourself, is our educational system prepared to meet the needs of its children? Is our approach to education relevant enough to capture the attention of Generation Z? Some may believe it is not the role of education to address the aforementioned societal ills. If not the school system, then what entity assumes such responsibilities?

Generation Z - Statistically Speaking

Researchers have provided a wealth of information about the state of America's children. Studies on the effect of children that have experienced child abuse and neglect, domestic violence, drug abuse, alcoholism, homelessness, parental mental illness, divorce, attention deficit disorder, with and without hyperactivity, and much more, provide a detailed picture of the resulting impact on our children. This manuscript simply uses this data to surmise the uncalculated collateral damage on our educational system and even more specifically, on classroom dynamics.

As you ponder the staggering numbers revealed in these studies, ask yourself, is our school system prepared for this underserved Generation Z? Conclusively, the failure is not in the preparation to educate, nor in the overall scope of education. It is the failure to know and acknowledge the audience as the most important part of the educational system. Who are the students today? Then ask how we can begin to ready ourselves to meet their overwhelming needs with the goal of decreasing the unfavorable impact on the educational system.

Child Abuse and Neglect

Approximately 3.3 million cases of child abuse are reported in the United States each year.[3] These numbers include neglect and abuse (sexual, physical, emotional, psychological and medical neglect) as defined by the department of Child Protective Services (CPS). Victimology extends throughout all cultures, ethnicities and economic statuses. According to the Center for Disease Control (CDC) nearly 1 in 4 girls and 1 in 6 boys will be sexually assaulted prior to their 18th birthday.[4] Researchers believe these numbers are immensely under reported due to the secrecy that shrouds abuse of children.

Perpetrators of such crimes are often known to the victim at an estimated 60% and an even greater tragedy is that approximately 30% of the perpetrators are family members.[5] Abuse patterns introduce a perpetual cycle that affects the educational system and the penal system at alarming rates. Prison studies reveal that 36% of all women and 14% of all men were abused as children.[6]

---

[3]Childhelp: "National Child Abuse Statistics",
<http//www.childhelp.org/pages/statistics?gclid=CI6GodCdrLICFQW>
(accessed April 2012).

[4] American Psychological Association: Child Sexual Abuse: What Parents Should Know, <http://www.apa.org/pi/families/resources/child-sexual -abuse.aspx> (accessed November 2012).

[5] Ibid

[6] Childhelp: "National Child Abuse Statistics,"
<http//www.childhelp.org/pages/statistics?gclid=CI6GodCdrLICFQW> (accessed April 2012).

The result of such abuse is as tragic as the act itself manifesting in depression, low self esteem, fear, guilt, social problems, sexualized behavior, substance abuse, suicide, *difficulty learning, and problems in school.*

Domestic Violence

Domestic violence occurs in 3 to 10 million homes yearly with children as eye witnesses.[7] According to the Department of Justice, domestic violence is a pattern of behavior, primarily abusive, where an individual seeks to gain control or exert power over the will of another. Overall, 10-20% of children are exposed to domestic violence.[8] Like sexual abuse, it is not bound by race, culture or economic status. This experience is most painful as it often involves both parents with whom the children share a bond. These violent acts destroy the sense of safety in the home environment and produce feelings of uncertainty. Family members live in a continuous cycle of panic and apprehension. This horrifying experience often leaves children feeling frightened and helpless. The effect on the child is so devastating that some researchers have associated Post Traumatic Stress Disorder (PTSD) as a result of domestic violence.

---

[7] National Center for Children Exposed to Violence, March 20, 2006, <http://www.nccev.org/violence/domestic.html> (accessed February 2012).
[8] Child Welfare Information Gateway, 2009, <http://www.childwelfare.gov/pubs/factsheets/domesticviolence.dfm> (accessed April 2012).

Sadly, children who witness domestic violence are also at risk of being physically abused in 30 to 60% of the same homes.[9] Even more exacerbating is the generational reoccurrence of these children perpetuating domestic violence. The American Psychological Association's Task Force on *Violence in the Family* (1996) reports that children witnessing the father's abuse of the mother is the greatest single risk factor for generational repeating of this behavior. Per the American Journal of Orthopsychiatry (1981), males who witness the abuse of their mothers are more likely to become abusers in adulthood.[10]

Students who witness domestic violence are greatly affected with signs manifesting such as depression, difficulty regulating emotions, fighting, bullying, *school truancy*, delinquency, substance abuse, early sexual activity, *low cognitive function, reduced intellectual competency, inability to concentrate* or *pay attention* in school, and *poor school performance*.[11] Some students refuse to attend school due to the embarrassment and shame. The effects of domestic violence appear in our classrooms daily and our focus remains the lesson plan rather than the student.

---

[9] Ibid

[10] Children and the Affects of Domestic Violence, <http://www.acadv.org/children.html > (accessed March 2012).

[11] American Family Physician-Medicine and Society: *Witnessing Domestic Violence: The Effects on Children*, <http://www.aafp.org/afp/2002/1201/p2052.html> (accessed May 2012).

Homelessness

The public school system experienced a 57% increase in the enrollment of homeless children in 2006-2007, during the recession. According to the National Coalition for the Homeless, September 2009 paper titled, *Education of Homeless Youth and Children,* four out of every two hundred children are currently homeless and that number will double.[12]   More current data indicates the highest number of 1,065,794 homeless students enrolled in 2010-2011.[13] This number, researchers confirm, is well under the true estimate for homeless children because many school districts have no reporting methods or requirements.

Homelessness as it is defined for children is the *lack of regular, fixed and adequate nighttime residence.*[14] Children residing in homeless shelters, transitional hotels, campgrounds, parks and short term facilities are considered homeless.   Causalities range from severe poverty to the lack of affordable housing in many regions. Studies reveal that 1.6 to 1.7 children have compulsory reasons to leave home such as violence, rape, drug abuse and such like.[15]   They too must be factored in the

---

[12] National Coalition for the Homeless, Washington, D.C: *Education of Homeless Youth and Children*, September 2009, <http://www.naehcy.org.fact.html> (accessed April 2012)

[13] National Association for the Education of Homeless Children and Youth: *Facts about Homeless Education*, <http://www.naehcy.org.fact.html> (accessed July 2012).

[14] Ibid

[15] Ibid

homeless youth count and provisions made to accommodate their specific needs within the school system.

The standard enrollment process can be a great barrier to education for the homeless. Proof of residency, when there is no residence, can be an extreme hurdle to overcome for enrollment. Maintaining health records, lack of transportation and multiple school transfers within a school year all represent great challenges to overcome for the homeless student. Many students fall further behind with every missed day of school in an attempt to acquire all that school registration requires.

It is extremely difficult to concentrate on education when your family is living in a car, sleeping outside, on a floor, or a couch. In other cases, children are living in an auditorium with 200 other strangers; only able to enter in the building after 6:00PM every evening, with no guarantee of an available cot. Moreover, shelters have a defined period of residence before the participant must leave. The end result is multiple school transfers within one school year for the affected students. The subsequent delay in records contributes to a tremendous number of days lost/absent from the educational process. *The typical outcome of repeated absences is academic failure.*

Recognizing the overwhelming challenges to education, the McKinney-Vento Homeless Assistance Act was passed to provide rights for this growing population. Rights include immediate enrollment without the necessary documents, transportation provided by the school to increase the probability of attendance, a homeless liaison in the school district and coordinators to insure the student's needs are met.

Incarceration

Another contributor to *Generation Z* is the child whose parent(s) is in the criminal justice system. Incarceration affects 1 out of 43 students in the United States between the ages of 13-17. Prison Fellowship offers the following astounding statistics[16]:

- There are more than 1.7 million children in the United States with an incarcerated parent (*The Sentencing Project/Research and Advocacy for Reform*, Feb. 2009). Some 10 million young people in the United States have had a mother or father - or both - spend time behind bars at some point in their lives (*Partnerships between Corrections and Child Welfare*, The Annie E. Casey Foundation, 2007).

- One in 43 (2.3 percent) American children has a parent incarcerated in state or federal prison (*Sentencing Project/Research and Advocacy for Reform*, Feb. 2009). Fifty-two percent of all incarcerated men and women are parents (*Sentencing Project*, 2009), and 75 percent of incarcerated women are mothers (*Incarcerated Parents and Their Children*, Bureau of Justice Statistics Special Report, 2000).

- Sixty-three percent of federal prisoners and 55 percent of state prisoners are parents of children under age 18 (*Incarcerated Parents and Their Children*, Bureau of Justice Statistics Special Report, 2000).

Fifty percent of inmates in the state and federal prison report not having received a visit from their children.[17] These same children suffer from the physical absence of the parent as well as a deep sense of loss resulting from no contact. The impact of incarceration on the family

---

[16] Prison Fellowship, <http://www.demossnewspond.com/pf/additional/statistics_concerning_childr en_of_prisoners> (accessed May 2012).

[17] Ibid

leads to financial problems, hardships and unstable family relationships.

The stigma and embarrassment of having an incarcerated parent causes students to suffer in silence withdrawing from social behaviors particularly those that might involve parental discussions. Some children lack an adequate support system and become wards of the state. In many cases their overall care and stability are compromised by constant moving and relocations. These are ingredients for *undisciplined behavior and poor academic performance.*

Having the privilege to mentor inside the correctional institutions for women, I have personally witnessed the emotional toll on the children of incarcerated women. Spanning a greater than three year period, I entered the prison with the visiting families and children. Mentorship was accomplished in the general population during family visitation hours. I was privy to discussions and conversations simply by virtue of close contact. Many of the family discussions were centered on the academic performance and behavior of the children. Along with the responsibility to mentor was an uninvited intrusion of emotions for the academic survival of the children of incarcerated parents.

The most compelling real life motion picture was in the eyes of the young children when their parent entered the visiting room. Surpassing the anticipation they experienced watching and staring through the bulletproof glass was the sheer fulfillment they experienced the moment they spotted their parent. Expressions of love, joy, excitement, hope, and forgiveness filled their faces. For as much as the surroundings would allow, they ran to greet their parent.

The older children and teenagers responded differently. While their eyes expressed love and care, their demeanor was far more reserved. Presumably filtered by their own age, understanding of the offense and their difficulty dealing with the punishment, they generally withheld outward displays of emotion.

While both age groups handled the initial greetings differently, they both handled departures the same. Tears, multiple hugs, and holding on were the common behaviors displayed. When multiple children from the same family visited, there appeared to be competition and even shoving of one another to get close to Mom. I overheard many reports by guardians and family members of the children not doing well in school. I witnessed the shame in their eyes and the lowering of their heads. Certainly on the visit to Mom, this was not the desired report they wanted her to have. I too felt their shame several tables over and heard their promises to do better.

Witnessing the child acting out toward the person who exposed their lack of educational achievement caused me to wonder if the weight of their emotions would allow them to honor their commitment to do better academically. In turn, I witnessed the hurt on Mom's face knowing that there was nothing she could do to be of service. Requests to try harder, behave better and study more were common responses. Those who understood their role as encourager followed such requests with a hug. Others focused on rehearsing the thought that the child should not be a problem to the caretakers.

Knowledge of personal suffering and emotional trauma infused my perspective rather than rebuke. After about the 20th visit, I began to ponder the eyewitness accounts of family dynamics and discussions about education that occurred in the visiting room. It became more of a curiosity and I began to study what the impact of incarceration might be on America's classrooms. Unbeknown to the local school system, any discussion about home life, the family tree, or getting parent signatures had the propensity to set off a chain reaction that educators are not typically trained to address.

Studies have revealed that children of incarcerated parents have *difficulty in school*. While imprisonment appears to be punishment of the criminal only, the outcomes are as far reaching as the classroom. This parental predicament can manifest in our schools as *unacceptable behaviors and discipline problems*. It can be further identified in *poor academic performance*. Oftentimes there is no support for educational issues in the absence of the parent.

Does our educational system account for, or prepare for, the impact of the judicial system on our educational system? While studies freely reveal the number of inmates in prison, are educators assessing the impact of the incarcerations on our school system? Are we prepared for the students whose parents are incarcerated and can provide no academic support?

Drug Abuse

In 2002, drug addiction and the resulting abuse cost an estimated 180.9 billion dollars in resource consumption, loss of productivity and premature death.[18] With numbers higher than any other preventable death, every fifteen minutes someone dies of a drug overdose in America.[19] As a major characteristic associated with child neglect and child abuse, drug and alcohol addiction is a significant risk factor whose impact has a direct effect on our school system. The *Child Help* organization reports that up to two thirds of all maltreatment cases site drug abuse as causative. Parents who abuse drugs and alcohol are three times more likely to abuse their children.[20] Due to behavioral modeling and mimicking behaviors, youths whose parent's abuse drugs are more likely to abuse drugs themselves.

Children of drug and alcohol abusers suffer shame, abandonment, guilt, and an inability to cope with life stressors. However, *parentification*, a new term by *Child Welfare* identified adolescents who have emerged to

---

[18] Office of National Drug Control Policy-Executive Office of the President, Fact Sheet: Consequences of Illicit Drug Use in America, December 2010, <www.whitehouse.gov/sites/default/files/ondcp/2012_ndcs.pd> (accessed May 2012).
[19] Ibid
[20] Ibid

assume the parental role in the family. They care for the children, address household duties and care for their parents who are often recovering from drug induced states. [21]

The unpredictable behavior of the drug abusing parent often results in the child missing significant periods of bonding and nurturing. The child subsequently develops defensive, protective and deceptive behaviors to protect themselves. To save themselves from the embarrassment of parental drug and alcohol abuse, they often preclude their parents from any parental functions. The resulting behaviors of adolescents whose parents abuse drugs are low self esteem, basic distrust of adult authority, *underdeveloped social skills, low academic performance*, and isolation.

The Center for Disease Control conducted a Youth Risk Behavior Surveillance in the United States in 2009. In monitoring major categories that lead to morbidity among the youth, they found drug and alcohol (72.5%) use as leading contributors. Drugs such as marijuana (36.8%), cocaine (6.4%), methamphetamines (4.1%), heroin (2.5%), ecstasy (6.7%), inhalants (11.7%), steroids (3.3%), hallucinogenic drugs (8.8%), injected drugs (2.1%) and prescription drugs (20.2%) without a

---

[21] How Parental Substance Use Disorders Affect Children, Chapter , 2009, <http://www.childwelfare.gov/pubs/usermanuals/substanceuse/chapterthree.cfm> (accessed May 2012).

prescription were fairly common among teens. [22] Certainly these results, in some fashion, affect student behavior in the classroom whether through *absenteeism, lack of participation or poor academic performance.* The connection is so definitive that the study urges comprehensive school health programs to address its findings.

Alcohol Abuse

While many studies combine alcohol and drug abuse, some have provided specific details for alcoholism significant enough to include in this manuscript. Children of those addicted to alcohol represent more than 28 million Americans with almost 40% of that number younger than 18.[23] Life in the home of an alcoholic is often characterized by tumultuous family conflict, physical abuse, emotional abuse, financial strain, and inadequate parenting. Families are also subject to recurrent relocation; therefore, stability is often lacking.

The National Association for Children of Alcoholics reports that male offspring are four times as likely to become an alcoholic and that alcoholism is the most

---

[22] Youth Risk Behavior Surveillance – United States 2009: Surveillance Summaries, Volume 59/SS-5, <http://www.cdc.gov/healthyyouth/yrbs/> (accessed April 2012).

[23] National Association for Children of Alcoholics (NACA): "Children of Addicted Parents: Important Facts," <http://www.nacoa.net/pdfs/addicted/pdf/> (accessed February 2013).

significant contributor to child abuse since 1986.[24] With statistics such as these, one can certainly ascertain that there is a much greater impact on academic performance than we currently know.

Comparison studies show strong links to conduct disorder and alcoholism. Children of alcoholics have increased rates of Attention Deficient Hyperactivity Disorder (ADHD) and Oppositional Defiant Disorder, low social skills, and challenged levels of self esteem. Academically, participants *scored low on achievement tests*; although, absenteeism and frequent transfers from relocations may also be a contributor to *low academic outcomes*.

Mental Illness

The National Alliance on Mental Illness (NAMI) reports that one in four adults suffer from a mental health challenge each year and one in 17, have a diagnosed serious mental illness.[25] As related to children, one in 10, have some form of mental illness.[26] Less than 33% of adults and less than 50% of children receive treatment for their mental disorder in the United States. The affects of

---

[24] Ibid

[25] National Alliance on Mental Illness (NAMI): "Mental Illness: Facts and Numbers," <http://www.nami.org/Template.cfm?Section=About_Mental_Illness&Template=/ContentManagement/ContentDisplay.cfm&ContentID=53155> (accessed September 2012).

[26] Ibid

mental illness on children, whether by the parents suffering, or their own, are devastating. These children in both their pre and post diagnostic state are seated in our classrooms. Our current teacher training is not geared toward recognizing or meeting their needs.

Children of the mentally ill and children with mental illness work to adapt to their environments both on and off school grounds. Some are more successful than others. Drug therapies are often used to help clients function with daily tasks. Common behaviors of children whose parents are mentally ill and children who have been diagnosed are maladaptive behaviors, *disruptive behaviors*, poor social skills, isolation and *poor academic performance.*

Divorce

According to the National Vital Statistics, viewing results from the year 2000 to 2011, over half of marriages in America end in divorce.[27] Numerous studies have reported the ill effects of divorce on children citing decreased household incomes, decreased health, *decreased educational performance which leads to a decrease in high school graduation rates and ultimately decreased college enrollment.* Divorce is a contributor to increased behavioral problems, increased emotional and

---

[27] National Vital Statistics System: "National Marriage and Divorce Rate Trends," <http://www.cdc.gov/nchs/nvss/marriage_divorce_tables.htm> (accessed March 2013).

psychological issues, as well as, increased cohabitation and drug use.

A study performed by Kent State University (Ohio) reported students from divorced households having *lower reading, spelling and math abilities* than non-divorced household children. *Grade retention* was also common among children of divorced parents.[28] Furthermore, a Cambridge University professor found that youth delinquency and adult criminal behavior's major culprit was parental divorce before the age of ten.[29]

Divorce usually results in a separation of family living quarters. Intact families move less frequently than divorced families. Relocation of broken families contributes to poor academic performance because the child not only faces the physical absence of the parent but also loses the home, neighborhood, school and friends with whom they are familiar. Relocation often contributes to lower performance because of the adjustment to a new living environment, new school, new teachers, and a new learning atmosphere.

With half of American marriages ending in divorce, it is highly conceivable that a similar percentage contributes to the behavioral and academic decline in our school systems. While divorce is a very personal choice, the collateral damage can be felt far beyond the home.

---

[28] Fagan, Patrick, PhD, World Congress of Families II: "The Effect of Divorce of Children," November 1999,
<http://www.worldcongress.org/wcf2_spkrs/wcf2_fagan.htm > (accessed May 2012).
[29] ibid

Studies have proven that divorce has long term effects on our educational, social and judicial systems. Generational outcomes have also been reported.

Attention Deficit Disorder (ADD) with & without hyperactivity (ADHD)

Attention deficit is one of the most commonly reported diagnoses among children. Three to seven percent of school children have Attention Deficit Disorder according to the Center for Disease Control (CDC).[30] Increasing at a rate of 5.5% per year since 2007, surveyed parents report approximately 10 % of children were diagnosed with ADHD.[31] Boys were two times more likely to be diagnosed than girls; recipients of Medicare had the highest rates of diagnoses.

The symptoms of ADD are inability to concentrate, easily distracted, inability to complete long term tasks, common misplacement of items, failure to make eye contact when spoken to, disorganized and forgetful. Students who have attention deficit with hyperactivity often appear anxious, fidgety, impulsive, and are extremely active during periods of expected inactivity.

The effects of ADD with and without hyperactivity have resulted in *higher grade failures, lower testing scores, behavioral challenges and higher rates for drop*

---

[30] Center for Disease Control (CDC), "Attention-Deficit/ Hyperactivity Disorder," <http://www.cdc.gov/ncbddd/adhd/data.html> (accessed April2012).
[31] Ibid

outs. The overall poor academic performance led to lower college completions results. The effects of ADHD are realized in our classrooms both behaviorally and academically.

Military Deployment

With our current military position, both parents can be deployed at the same time leaving the children parentless. It is no surprise that children of parents in the armed services contribute to Generation Z in that their natural attention span often focuses on the loved one deployed to battle fields or foreign lands. They are often moved from their homes to live with extended family while their parents serve in the military.

While studies have shown a significant correlation between *low test scores* and deployment of greater than 19 months for elementary and middle school students, data does not bear the same outcomes for high school students of deployed military personnel.[32] However, *less completion of homework, an increase in absenteeism, and gaps in academic requirements* resulting from relocations, are highly related to deployments.

The Rand Corporation Study found that during deployment male students tended to show more aggression and anger, while female students showed more

---

[32] Rand Corporation, "Effects of Soldiers Deployment on Children's Academic Performance and Behavioral Health," <http://www.rand.org/content/dam/rand/pubs/monographs/2011/RAND_MG1 095.pdf> (accessed September 2012).

depression and risk taking behaviors such as sexual promiscuity and cutting.[33] The absence of the deployed parent was a major contributor to the behavioral outcomes outlined.

Intrinsic to every child are basic desires for safety and survival. Who will love me? Where will I live? What will I eat? Who will care for me? Who will encourage me? Who will help me? Our education system has accepted the mantle for, "Who will educate me?" However, due to the complexity of the student body, it simply has to offer more.

Generation Z has an incalculable impact on the educational system that, among other things, causes it to appear ineffective. Extenuating life situations, conditions and circumstances provided generation Z with the reasons to check out of the education process. With a composite aggregate of the aforementioned studies, statistically speaking, in a class size of approximately 35 students, approximately 12 to 16 students are either emotionally, cognitively, socially or behaviorally challenged by their personal life circumstances.

Painstakingly obvious was the recurring outcomes from each study citing low cognitive functioning, problems in school, poor academic performance, low self esteem, risky sexual behavior, and inability to control emotions. While the studies point directly to perceived societal ills, the outcomes have a direct effect on the

---

[33] Ibid

children who occupy our classrooms, thus the school system itself.

Most challenging are the generational cycles that feed addiction, domestic violence drug abuse and incarceration. *Without question, societal ills greatly affect our educational system and our inaction greatly affects society.* Therefore, our solutions must be broader than the standard educational structures, procedures and systems.

While certainly not true of all students in the aforementioned situations, Generation Z is often present in class, but absent in mind. They are deeply challenged in relation to their focus on education. The aforesaid studies strongly present the correlation that the greater the challenges experienced by *Generation Z, the* greater the impact on the overall educational system.

Our current educational system must shift its focus and prepare to serve those who enter our doors with the same laser sharp precision used to plan the *smart classroom.* The student must become the focus of our preparation, more than the tools we use to instruct the occupant of the classroom. That which is natural must come first. Similarly, a hungry student must be fed before we can teach him/her. Our system must expand its current services to incorporate meeting the natural and social needs of its student body. It must also openly communicate about the extenuating circumstances that students may be facing while directing them to the proper help within the school's expanded scope of services.

It is the goal of this sharing to introduce and emphatically declare that Generation Z is worth every effort toward inclusion. They deserve the inalienable right to education. More than emphasizing classroom tools and books, we must provide the bridge that these students can successfully cross and become active participants in the learning process. This bridge building process may include entities outside the normal scope of education; however, they can easily become a part of the normal prevue of education without removing the student from the educational environment.

My experiences with Generation Z have greatly broadened my scope of our nation's educational responsibilities. Along with reading, writing and arithmetic, we have the responsibility to pay attention to the details. More than names on the roll, these are lives that present themselves five days a week. They are present, in our care, more than any place other than home; therefore, schools have the greater opportunity to bring services within the educational borders.

Continue this high school journey through the eyes of a 51 year old. Allow me to introduce you to Generation Z. It is my hope that these experiences may be as life changing for you as they were for me.

Experiences with Generation Z

During my tenure as a high school student, I realized how much I did not know in relation to the real challenges of high school students today. My every reference and exchange was framed by my personal experience which was approximately three decades old. Before this boot camp, no one could have told me that high school had changed that much or that my understanding was wrong. I was wrong.

By the end of week two, I was apologizing to my child for my own lack of knowledge and outdated perceptions of school that have ruled our exchanges for years. "Well I know school has not changed that much," was my customary response. Now I simply utter, "Things have changed." I listen with greater intensity and far more patience today because I am learning and no longer consider myself having learned.

The unplanned, unprompted exchanges that occurred with Generation Z changed my perspective as a parent and an educator forever. Parental involvement is so necessary and currently nil, with the exception of sports and booster clubs. We have been absent from the classroom for far too long. In an effort to compliment me, one retired substitute commented that in her 20 years of teaching, I was the first parent she had seen in the classroom. She thanked me for being there. I was embarrassed. In disbelief, I wondered, where were we and where had we been? We have come to the games, but not to the classroom, which should be the primary purpose of enrollment and involvement.

I gladly share these exchanges with Generation Z in hopes that you might see the necessity of parental involvement and the hope that exists in this generation and every generation to come.

An Unforgettable Meeting -Trina Z

There she was, as attractive as possible in her well figured frame. She sported a tremendous personal style, a beautiful bright smile, and a head full of wavy brown hair. The boys swarmed around her like bees. For some unexplained reason, our eyes met. "Hi, Mrs. Jay's Mom," she said with a big smile.

Pleasantly surprised that she knew my name, I responded, "Hi. How are you?"

"I am Trina Z," she said.

"Hi Trina Z, pleased to meet you." I wanted to shake her hand but missed the opportunity because of all the boys crowding around her. I also thought it best that I refrain from touching any student while on the grounds. I never wanted my presence to be misunderstood. A smile would have to be enough.

"I want you to know that Jay is always mean to me," she playfully stated.

"No I'm not," with defensive surprise responded Jay.

"Jay you know better than that. I will take care of him. My parenting job is just not finished," I played along smiling.

"Jay, you are going to get it," Trina Z echoed.

"If he treats you mean tomorrow let me know," I said with assurance that things would change.

"I will!" she said, excited at the prospect that she may have caused Jay some trouble.

As we held this conversation I could not help but notice the way the boys were pulling on her and trying to touch her. She was pulling away but that did not stop them from making advances. I felt the need to rescue her because the advances were not pure in nature. Resisting the urge to pull her near me as I passed by, I prayed a simple prayer: "God if it is your will for me to help her or to be of service, please make a way for it to happen without me breaking any rules".

I resisted the urge to rescue her as though she were my own child and trusted God to grant me an opportunity to encourage her. I was careful not to do anything that could cause harm to the school or its students. I trusted that if my visit had another purpose, opportunity to fulfill it would come. I had to be patient and wait on it. The opportunity did not come that day, but it surely came several weeks later.

Trina Z caught my attention in the classroom because it was clear that her personal preoccupation was not education. It was something totally different. There were many days of getting up and walking around the classroom from restlessness and sheer boredom. The noisy sighs, loud comments about this boring class, and inattention were just a few signs that tipped me off.

Then it happened. Few parents or teachers were prepared for what I witnessed. When Trina Z entered the classroom, I noticed that her doubled tank top was very revealing. The only thing covered was the areola (nipples). I am guessing between 36-38 sized breasts, were half exposed by the top she wore. That was not the most shocking thing. Someone had written on each of her breasts in permanent black marker. There was no writing on her neck or chest, simply upon each of her breasts. My heart broke.

I began to wonder about Trina Z's self image. How low it must be to allow someone to write on your breast and you publically display it. Equally as grievous was thinking about the mind of the person who disrespected her to that extent. Why would she allow that to happen? What bothered me more was that this was 4th period and she had not been sent to the office. Was this behavior considered okay?

My prayer was even more earnest this time. It was from a broken and contrite heart. I wanted to cry for her but this was not the time or the place to do so. She greeted me with a smile as always and I did the very same for her. Careful not to show disappointment but watching for opportunity, I began to focus on the class. In an unusual move, I remained on campus that day until 6th period. Periodically, I would remember the situation with Trina Z, but my overall demeanor was one of sadness; however, I was still in prayer. I kept reminding myself to speak the truth in love. I cautioned myself to remember that this is someone's child and my words must be building blocks, not destroyers. Then it happened. Just as I was leaving the campus coming down the second story stairwell, there she was.

Trina Z with all her breast writings still had not been sent to the office. I looked around to see what rules I might be violating, happily there were none. We were eye to eye. I smiled as bright as I could and said, "Trina you are a beautiful, smart and brilliant young woman. I have been watching you in the classroom and you can be anything you desire. You have personality and charisma and I believe you will be successful." Then I asked the question, "Do you want to be successful?" Yes was her answer. "Then there is one thing I must share. As long as you draw attention to areas below your neck, no one will know about the tremendous mind you have above your neck. Make them know you, not your assets. Draw attention to your mind, not your chest. One will get you where you want to be and the other will not." She looked me directly in the eyes and said, "Yes Ma'm." I completed my talk by saying, "And by the way, permanent marker can be removed with isopropyl alcohol."

Just as we completed our conversation, another Caring Teacher walked up and said, "Who did this to you? If you were in my class today, this would have come off. Go get a jacket and cover up."

I chimed in to say, "I just informed her that alcohol will remove permanent marker." The Caring Teacher thanked me but went on to tell the student, "I expect better from you."

Teach Because I Came!

Why did I call this particular teacher a caring teacher? During breaks for lunch and possible assemblies, I would visit the Caring Teacher's class. She is one who goes beyond the call of duty for her students. Her story is in a later chapter titled my *Experiences with Educators*. She also responded to the writing on the breast as I hoped someone in authority would.

The painfulness of that day stuck with me for a while. My heart ached for all our children. It is your child's unknown actions and behaviors that hinder parenting for good parents. It is about what you do not know that your children are doing that keeps you from correcting it. I hoped I helped a parent with the unknowns that day.

Trina Z was one student. However, she was a type of all students; young, impressionable and easily misguided. To what extent, I will never know. However what shocked me the most about Trina Z was not that day, it was the days that followed.

On our next class meeting, Trina Z was dressed in a very preppy outfit with a collared blouse, respectable length skirt and jacket. She wore personality glasses that made her look like the smartest person in the room. Her entire demeanor had changed. She participated in class, answered questions and volunteered to help the teacher (who previously bored her). I could not have been more proud than if she were my own child. What a tremendous transformation! When I walked in our eyes met. She spoke as always. This time I said, "I love the new look. It becomes you." She continued this style of dress throughout my visits. She also continued to participate in class, competitively trying to earn all the extra credit points.

Oftentimes, adults give counsel to students and we have no idea if it is received or rejected. This experience clearly demonstrated that the value to the recipient is directly determined by the condition of the heart when counsel is given. Scolding, disapproving and belittling just do not produce the right fruit, even if the situation appears to deserve that response. It became abundantly clear to me that the right opportunity to speak with Trina Z did not present itself until my motives and purpose of heart were pure. It was simply hope for her future as a young maturing woman that drove my desire to speak with her. My care was unconditional. My hope for her future was without limits. It caused me to hurt like a parent does when they see *their* child misbehaving. Then it was necessary to put emotion aside and work on the future of this child without condemning her for the past few hours. Only then can God do his best work.

Whatever happened to cause the much needed transformation not only blessed Trina Z's life, but it began to slowly transform the lives of other students around her. The ones who openly spoke of their boredom in history class were now opening their books and trying to earn extra credit points in competition with Trina Z. Indescribable joy is the only way to surmise my emotions after this experience. Ironically, the very thing that saddened me in days prior eventually allowed me to experience great joy.

I will never know if Trina Z's parents knew of her actions that day or how many other caring citizens spoke with her; however, I think they would be proud to know that she responded to counsel, received instructions and demonstrated a positive result. The measure of a good student is not that they are without error or without mistake, but that they are wise enough to rise from their mistakes in judgments and make great strides forward.

It was at this moment as I watched her progress that I realized this assignment to return to high school was greater than my understanding and had far reaching implications. It was no longer about my child but about our children. My vision became clearer, not in terms of eyesight but in terms of possibility.

The Curser

My next Algebra II session was even more enlightening than the previous lightweight student revolt. The Einstein teacher was absent and a substitute was in the class when we arrived. She was somewhat witty and a bit self absorbed. As the class progressed, I was sure she, too, knew her Algebra.

She began the class by introducing herself and sharing her personal achievements. She highlighted her degrees and the degrees of her family, including her husband and children. It was clear she was impressed with where the degrees were obtained. She was retired and loved math so much that she was a substitute for the school system. She enjoyed teaching whenever she could. Then, more damaging than the previous information, she presented the straw that broke the camel's back. All this was accomplished within the first five minutes of the class.

"Look at the board," she said. "Do you see all the writing on these two white boards?

"Yes," some of the students replied.

"Well, this is how much you will need to write to solve *one* problem on your work sheet that Mr. Einstein left for you."

I looked up. Clearly there was writing over every inch of those two six-foot white boards. I had assumed this was the answers to their homework the night before.

Surely she would follow the pattern and classroom order of the Einstein teacher and cover homework first.

"What!" The students gasped.

I gasped myself, took a deep breath, and shook my head. I had hoped to learn Algebra II that day. I had hoped a fresh female perspective would pave the way to understanding. It was obvious that realization of my hope would not be obtained that day. Did the Einstein teacher slip in his Mom as the substitute?

I became interested in seeing how she would recover from this off putting introduction. Presentation can be everything. Just the appearance of the amount of work was staggering. It was about to blow everything the students, including me, might learn.

The visual was mentally challenging and left you feeling like you were in an episode of the discontinued TV program *Numbers*. Was she serious? The students mumbled a bit then they reviewed the handout for the assignment. She handed me a copy and I thanked her. My real thoughts were quite different. I looked at the problems again. The length alone was a problem for me.

I wondered if she had learned in teacher training about the value of the visual. If so, she might have used it differently. Starting with a clean board, together they could have solved the problems, with class input. This inclusive method could have sharpened their skills, caused spontaneous review and possibly fill in some gaps. Being sure to encourage the students as they labored together to solve the problems could have catapulted her to the *Best Substitute Ever,* simply because she engaged the learner in a tedious task rather than overwhelmed them.

The *One Sided Approach* to education, *I have already done the work, just copy it or read it,* fails to produce anyone's best. It is a presentation. A presentation requires more work from the presenter, requires more to keep the students interest and requires no work from the recipient. This was certainly not interactive.

There are greater ways to use the visual. The students could have accomplished what was assigned had she invited them to work on the solution together. At the end, the class could look back to see what they had accomplished. From this perspective the visual becomes a congratulatory mark rather than one to begin the journey.

As to be expected, our Curser, began to curse and talk openly about his need to understand. This time he took his conversation a little further and openly discussed that he should have stayed with the teacher he had last year. Per his admission, he was the better teacher. He followed that with a few expletives.

Mind you, the substitute teacher had not taught anything up to this point. Questions that she received from students who attempted to solve the worksheet were answered by directing them to sections of the two six-foot white boards. She moved quickly from table to table answering questions, pointing to the white boards, attempting to extinguish the fires from disgruntled students.

Then it happened. The two tables directly in front of me put down their pencils and began to talk. One of the very studious females remarked that she had never seen this work before in her life. She began to rub her head and sigh. Almost in tears, they began to discuss how they needed this class to graduate.

At that moment, I was reminded that there was more than one way to solve these equations. What the Substitute had on the board obviously was a different way. My son was being tutored by a mathematician who taught him wonderful short cuts to solving algebraic problems. He shared them with his teacher, who confirmed that there are multiple ways to solve algebraic equations. This had to be the longer way.

Without warning, the students turned to me again asking, "Do you understand this part?" My answer was the same. I just offered it on a different day. "I am sorry, I do not."

Two tables ahead, a young lady shared, "I asked my parents for help and they don't understand either. My brother graduated from college and he cannot help me. He took Algebra II and got A's. But he said the way they teach it today, he does not understand. I cannot get help at school and I cannot get help at home." Another student shared, "My parents don't even speak the language. So there is no one to help me."

I was impressed by their openness and felt compelled to help in some way. My train of thought was interrupted by the Curser. He was attempting to do the work. Then, throwing down his pencil in frustration, he espoused profanity.

I looked up and asked God, "Is this my project. Is this my time?" I sensed a peace and a readiness to take the necessary steps. I prayed for the right words and to be an encouragement. When I lifted up my eyes, the Curser was looking at me. I waited to see if it were a chance glance. He continued to stare with his eyes fixed on me.

"Okay, Okay, I get the hint," I mumbled then signaled for him to come to me. The substitute was roaming from table to table and not aware of my request. With no objection, he rose and came before me.

In a private conversation I shared, "You are an extremely bright young man. I have noticed how you are able to follow along with Mr. Einstein as he goes over problems. You have the basics and you can do this. You have most of the tools. There are some areas that you need a little more help, but I am certain you can get it. There are a few things you might have to do to be successful in this class."

"What do I need to do?" He was eager to know.

"First, you would have to stop talking long enough to hear the entire solution. Did you know that it is impossible to learn if you are talking while the teacher is talking?" I quizzed.

"No, I did not know that," conceded the Curser.

"Secondly, choose a more appropriate language. The cursing does not go along with the bright future you will have. You are a brilliant young man. You do not want your choice of language to destroy your opportunities before they begin. Can you do that for you?"

"Yes Ma'm, I can," he said confidently.

"I know you can. Thank you Son."

"Thank you, Ma'm," he uttered as he went back to his seat.

We had a moment in time. It was for this reason our paths crossed. We never spoke directly to each other again. However, I can certainly say that I never heard another curse word from this young man during my visits. He never spoke disrespectfully in class after that conversation. He governed himself for the good of his class. His obedience eventually helped the other students at his table simply because he was no longer a distraction.

I delayed exiting the classroom to thank the substitute teacher for her time. I pondered whether to share how overwhelming the board displays were to the students at the tables nearby and to me. I decided to hold my thoughts.

She thanked me for being there and said I was the first parent she had seen in a classroom in 20 years of teaching. I was shocked and saddened. She then opened the door and asked if I had any comments about the class that day.

She asked, so I shared. I complimented her helpful manner. I appreciated how she attempted to get to every student who had a question. I explained that she might not have to work so hard if she allowed the students to participate in solving the problem. Then it would be more of an achievement for them rather than a daunting task.

She responded by saying that the students did not have the basic tools to understand what she was teaching. She added that they lacked basic skills. My personal disappointment grew. Mr. Einstein said that these were basic skills from Algebra I and that if the students did not know them, they should not be in his class. Now the substitute is saying the same thing. So who teaches the skills that they lack? Whose job is it to fill in the gaps?

The time of my visitation was the third quarter of the school's four grading quarters. How could an entire class, with the exception of one, be pushed through three grading periods and not have the basic skills? Were the basic skills ever reviewed? The question remains. Who is driving the learning experience? Is it the preplanned curriculum, the teacher's lesson plan, or the student? Clearly something was awry.

I concur that every student will not find math an enjoyable subject and the evidence will show up in the grade. I understand that all students do not learn at the same pace. What I reject is the notion that students cannot master basic skills and even excel. I further object to educators who pronounce their inability BEFORE they teach. This substitute simply handed out a worksheet and pointed at the board. Had she taught them, some skills may have been learned.

Acknowledging her years of experience in the classroom, I looked into her eyes and said, "I respectfully disagree. These students can learn the necessary skills. They want to learn them. In my time of being here, I am waiting to see someone veer away from the lesson plan and teach them." She was stunned by my comments. I too was stunned by hers. The definition that I learned of teaching is that it is repeating and repeating until learning takes place. I was waiting for someone to begin teaching.

The Sharers

Not long after we had our first child, I can remember my mother-in-law saying to me, "Don't ever say what your children won't do." After she said it I almost became offended until I thought about all that I did in my youthfulness that my parents never knew and still have no idea of today. Things can happen right under your nose, while you are present, and as parents and teachers, you are none the wiser. Furthermore, each generation has new intrigues, distractions, interests and perspectives. Our older experiences loom in our minds and overshadow the possibility of new nuances.

My generation survived without much technology (Ipods, Ipads, ITouch and the internet). To the best of my knowledge telephones, television and radio were as far as we had progressed. We even lacked the foresight that such tools could exist. What can be accomplished with these electronic marvels is beyond my comprehension and comfort zone some days. Yet this generation, for which it was developed, has adapted so easily that they cannot see productivity without it. Should you question their mental acuity, simply time them sending a text, tweet, or downloading music or an APP. Then time yourself. As an eyewitness to the misapplied brilliance of this generation, with the correct focus, I am certain they will achieve much more.

One of the most startling things that I experienced during my recent high school tenure was the overwhelming "copying" or "sharing" of information that took place among students. In times past, this same activity was called *cheating*. The magnitude of the problem was widespread and could compete with a Xerox copier. It was present in almost every class I attended, occurring each time that I was present. Overwhelmed by the outpouring of evidence, I began to study the process.

It was difficult to subdue the urge to raise my hand and say, "You have a multitude of people passing around someone's work." More directly, I could have simply said, they are *cheating*. My hesitation was not only in the fact that I could not identify anyone by name, but the network was so slick, there would be no evidence to corroborate my findings. The more I observed and studied the process, the more amazed I was at how the students worked together. Interestingly enough, the process began at the onset of the assignment and continued until the bell rang.

My memory recalls, with great certainty, asking a classmate how they solved a problem that I deemed difficult or if they'd found an answer I could not. I always attempted to do the work on my own. There were times that a friend filled the gap on the bus to school. Never would I consider this cheating, but more like helping one another.

Somehow in the most perverted way the progression moved from helping someone to doing it for them or allowing them to copy *all* the answers. In their own minds, with admission, they were helping one another.

The Network

Without forewarning I witnessed an astounding and intricate network among students in four of the five classes I shadowed. Students had become so well versed on the habits of the teachers that they developed ways to achieve their own agenda. They managed to avoid detection, even if the teacher was walking around the room. These were different students in different classes, and some were in different grades. The classes ranged from college prep to state testing courses.

To my chagrin, my presence was no deterrent to the network they had established. In all honesty, I witnessed this behavior several times before I understood what I was viewing. Once certain of the startling details, I became a private eye, trying to learn all that I could. My suspicions were later confirmed as truth in an unsolicited discussion with a student.

In utter shock and amazement, I beheld a bold and brazen generation at work. Clearly this was a preexisting infrastructure, well established before I became an eyewitness, with networking so organized it could put most corporations to shame. Either I had the best seat in the house or the activity was so well practiced that the well trained eye could miss it. With the precision of a kleptomaniac the activities described below began.

The teacher gave an assignment such as the chapter question in the book or a worksheet. The person who studied, paid attention, and hopefully knew the work, completed the assignment as quickly as possible. Once finished, that individual would get up holding two sheets of paper (held to appear as one sheet). The overall scheme operated under the shroud of the student submitting completed assignments in the teacher's inbox. As the student approached the front, another student in the network would cough or ask the teacher a question, to create a distraction. During the distraction, while approaching the front, the student who appeared to be submitting their work accidentally dropped the blank paper on the floor. While bending to pick up the dropped sheet, the completed assignment was covertly placed on the table of the next person designated to copy the assignment. When the first student reached the front, if the teacher was looking in their direction, the blank sheet of paper was put in the inbox. If the teacher was distracted, the blank paper was thrown in the nearest trashcan. The initial person did not submit their assignment, though it appeared as such.

The second student, who clandestinely received the ill gotten work, quickly placed it under their paper and copied very quickly (30-60 seconds) without reading a single question or checking an answer. Their paper was then passed to the third person at their table.

Once the third person received the paper, the second student would rise with two sheets of paper heading toward the front, supposedly to submit their work. A student would create a distraction as the second student moved forward. With the second student's paper being copied by others at the table, they assumed the responsibility of placing the work of the first student in the teacher's box. Careful to remove the blank sheet of paper from the teacher's inbox, submitted by student one, the process did not arouse suspicion. The blank sheet of paper was carefully disposed of before anyone was aware.

The third person continued the cycle as other classmates were cued to create the next distraction. At times there would be multiple people copying from the same paper, then creating a distraction as they got up to deliver the copied work to the next table. This network continued daily with homework and in-class assignments. I was not present on test days; however, the boldness of the network that I witnessed would not hesitant to find a way to get answers. My reservations were confirmed when I sat in a class where the covert cheating network went undetected.

Surprisingly, in a class that I personally enjoyed, I did not detect the covert cheating network. Signals may have been missed because my seat was in the front, rather than in the back. Nonetheless, I considered my observance of students equally as diligent. The teacher announced that she was retesting the students because of an incident with cheating. She indicated that the problem was so widespread that the only recourse was to create a new test. As she distributed the new exam, she encouraged the students to trust their own ability to study and learn material. The craftiness of the operation was so slick that it was undetected, with me present and knowledgeable of the signs.

Kudos and congratulations to the students who refused to participate in the covert operation. Their integrity is to be admired and applauded. Aware of the network, but unwilling to participate, students with character labored over the assignments. Their moral prowess did not fail to present itself by their refusal to touch the ill gotten work slipped onto their table, nor would they look in its direction. Instead, they looked away until the intended party removed it from their work area.

Pure conjecture would espouse that teachers were lazy and never got up from their desk, otherwise they would have known about this network taking place under their noses. Shamefully, much of this operation took place while teachers were up, walking around, helping students and answering questions. Some found it interesting that students were able to finish so quickly, but for the most part, teachers were none the wiser.

In their defense, rarely, if ever, does a teacher have the opportunity to sit in the back of their own classroom and observe. Most of their work is conducted from the front with instruction, grading and other administrative tasks. Most teachers certainly walk to the back of their classroom but rarely does the opportunity exist to stay in the back and simply observe.

Calculating the Loss

Amazingly organized and excruciatingly dishonest, this covert network represents an incalculable loss to our nation. Moreover, it is a glaringly painful manifestation of loss, both past and present, with devastating implications to our future.

Students who participate in such operations have very low self esteem and have lost the willingness to trust their own ability to learn. Repeated academic failures, lack of respect for the educational system, and misplaced values gave birth to this system. Clearly these students demonstrated a greater level of appreciation, trust and respect for the mind of the person from whom they copied rather than their own. The blind trust was so deep, that students did not read any questions, or check any answers to confirm correctness. They copied copiously in hope of a passing grade.

Lack of respect for their own abilities was so great that the fear of exposure, reprimand, and expulsion did not factor into their value system. I hurt for them. Some saw me looking but did not have the courage to stop the madness or were simply willing to chance getting caught. Those involved lacked character and overlooked the value of personal integrity. Character and integrity are not part of the school's curriculum; however, they are critical to a successful life.

More painful to this elaborate scheme were the unimaginable missed opportunities for learning. Copying someone else's work added no value to their lives or their educational experience. No knowledge was gained but a great amount of self respect was lost. School was never designed to waste the entire day copying like a Xerox machine. Who is occupying our classrooms?

A great contributor to failure in the school system begins with who occupies the seat, even more so than who is teaching. Both roles are critical to the educational process but honest, hardworking students can cause any teacher to improve their teaching skills. Likewise committed, hardworking teachers can cause students to raise their level of commitment to their own education. Somewhere along the line, the value of education has been lost. This value has not been replaced by something of greater value but by electronic devices that students do not need, nor can they afford.

In one day I witnessed students constantly asking for help because they want to learn Algebra II. Later that same day I uncover a network so popular and intricate, that the participants have no idea they are contributing to their own destruction. There was much to ponder and to determine what to do.

The cycle continued through almost ten to fifteen students. The process was complete in seconds and making it nearly impossible to catch anyone in the act. If this was the practice for homework and in class assignments, I shuddered at the thought of what could happen during a test.

Baby Doll Z – Present But Not Really

History, the fourth class of the day was truly a collection of characters. The personalities of the students were quite strong; however, the teacher was soft spoken, polite and respectful. She did exactly what teachers were taught to do. Her lesson plans were always prepared. Her power point presentations were colorful and pleasing to the eye. She gave notes often from the power point presentations and she was working her assignment respectfully. One student whom I call Baby Doll Z was determined to be a thorn at every class meeting. It seemed that the more the teacher tried to reach her students, Baby Doll Z was determined to cause a scene and undermine the learning process.

Baby Doll Z was not fond of history class. How do I know? She said so loudly and repeatedly. With expression and emotion, Baby Doll Z blurted out, "I hate this class! It is so b-o-r-i-n-g! Man I hate coming here. It makes me mad!" She would get up from her seat, prance around and demand the restroom pass.

I was always amazed at the level of respect that the teacher demonstrated toward Baby Doll Z. She did so unconditionally and without regard to the level of disrespect she was receiving. While I found the student's behavior appalling, I found the teacher to be commendable. I was proud of her. There were times that I shook my head wondering how I would handle such rudeness. I was not sure I could attain the level of calm and mildness of response when under such great attack. She did so faithfully.

Baby Doll Z was model thin and extremely attractive. Her makeup was always perfect, her designer clothes, designer handbag and shoes all matched. My first impression was brunette glamour girl. I noted the well manicured hands and feet and pondered the investment someone was making in this child. Occasionally her cell phone emerged from the handbag so that she could stay in the know. With that said, there was an unmistakable restlessness about Baby Doll Z.

Baby Doll Z entered the room with an automatic desire to exit. She politely requested the restroom pass each meeting within the first 5 minutes. One day she was denied the pass due to the pattern of abuse she had set. Her resulting frustrations were openly shared. Her tone, demeanor and posture indicated that she would not be denied the opportunity to go to the restroom in spite of what the teacher said. Her banter was exhausting even for me as an observer. Eventually she was sent to the office. Honestly, I am not sure she ever made it to the office as many times as she was sent. Baby Doll Z just did not demonstrate an ability to follow instructions.

In recollection, when the restroom pass was granted, Baby Doll Z returned as ornery as before she left. She never joined the learning process before or after her restroom exit. She was completely and utterly preoccupied with life outside the classroom. My mind wondered what caused a young woman to be that angry for so long. How does even the most prepared teacher address this scenario?

Baby Doll Z was seated within arm length of my area. The angry outbursts, frustrations and constant sighing were all part of her daily drama. My parental presence in the back meant nothing to her because she often glared in my direction as she passed by on her tirades. Her disrespect for adult authority was openly displayed and duly noted. She successfully challenged me as a former educator and parent. I did observe while trying not to show emotion or feed her frenzy.

Baby Doll Z was enrolled as a student in this high school; however, in her mind she was no student. In the six-weeks of observance for this particular class, Baby Doll Z did not pull out a single pen or pencil, nor did she open the bejeweled notebook she held in her arms. She had school supplies but she had not come for school. Whatever distracted her had such a significant pull, she no longer tried to learn, at least not while I was present. The value of her education had not become clear to her.

While I did not have the privilege to spend any personal time with Baby Doll Z, I had the privilege to spend time with her history teacher. Our exchange was simply remarkable and witnessing the change in the history class was nothing short of amazing. Our story is shared in the section titled, *Making History – Working Together*. Nonetheless, it was clear that teacher training and certification had not prepared this otherwise good teacher to work with difficult students.

For clarity, it is important to note that I prayed for Baby Doll Z just as I had for the Curser and Trina Z. Neither time nor opportunity was granted to me; therefore, I accepted that my assignment would not entail private encounters with every situation I deemed necessary. I also understood that everything had a season and this was not the season for Baby Doll Z and me. I hoped that someone else would sow into her life, and that like the Curser, this behavior did not appear in every class.

Sexuality and Generation Z

Call me naive, but it never crossed my mind that my child could or would be sexually harassed in high school. Obviously the school systems are well aware and attempt to avert such behavior through assemblies and videos explaining the details and the penalties associated with it. Each student was required to sign a paper of awareness and acknowledgment. I can remember this process being followed even while my student was in middle school. This was great, but I did not understand the impetus behind it until I attended high school myself.

As I journeyed from class to class, I noticed quite a few faces locked together. I was surprised at the close bodies swaying with no air between them. This action took place along the walls of many classroom buildings. Though 2500 other students, plus teachers and faculty were in the near vicinity, these individuals were in a world of their own. The phrase "get a room" was appropriate for some.

What I witnessed is represented in the polls conducted by the CDC in 2011 of high school students. Almost half, 47.4% were sexually active. Over 76% of the sexually active did not use any form of protection or prevention. The overwhelming burden of such action or inaction is that over 400,000 women between the ages of 14-19 gave birth in 2009.[34] I knew of teenage pregnancy, I simply did not associate the school environment as a breeding ground for promiscuous behavior. A really involved parent would know the sexual pressures that befell their student as they entered the campus. It was at this very point that I declined the title "involved parent." I was beyond head in the sand. I was simply ignorant to the daily pressures of high school.

I can remember standing in the middle of the quad and turning in circles, looking lost but simply trying to assess how many couples I could spot in the midst of what I used to call *puppy love* but now deem as foreplay. Then I paused to determine who was minding the store. The fox was in the hen house and nobody was squealing.

Everyone was working, there were no slackers on this campus. The security staff was busy responding to calls on the quads. They were running to check restrooms after the bell to make sure students were in a class by the time of the tardy bell. Teachers were ushering students into their classroom and busy monitoring the activity both inside and outside the room. Who had time to keep the young lovers focused on school? Whose job was it to instill personal respect and dignity so that public heavy petting was not an eyesore? Whose job was that?

_____

[34] Center for Disease Control and Prevention, Sexual Risk Behavior: HIV, STD, & Teen Pregnancy Prevention, July 2011, <www.cdc.gov/HealthyYouth/**sexualbehaviors**> (accessed June 2012).

Reality sat in. I had not seen so many locked lips in all my life, not even after two weeks in Paris, France. I thought Paris was for *lovers,* but high school was accelerating to first place at the speed of a racecar driver. I was an eye witness.

Science clearly informs us that hormones are raging during this stage of development. World and the nightly news are constantly informing us that sexuality among the young is at an all time high. Some schools are passing out condoms. Clinics give them away free. Even though society is sounding the alarm, as parents we may be sitting at home thinking that high school was like it was in our day. A few students were sexually active. Our hope is that our child is not one of the few and that they know better.

Here I was, an eye witness simply shocked at the emblazoned public display of affection. Hand placement had risen to a new low. Hands on the buttocks, then hands sliding between the legs were an alarming visual. If this was the depth of public affection being displayed on the high school campus in broad daylight, with an audience, one need not imagine what private moments entailed.

Then it hit me. Admittedly I felt completely out of touch with this high school generation. My concept of high school was not the same as high school today. I had only associated school with teaching, learning, grades, college advancement, and sports. I failed to address the social interactions and the implications of them? Was I so well versed in what my high school reality was that I was blinded by what their high school reality is? Had I paid real attention, my prayers would have been different. They would have gone far beyond successful completion of tests/quizzes and respecting authority. I would have prayed for wisdom, strength and courage to stand for what was right. I would have prayed for good friends, not virtual ones. I would have done so many things differently. As it was, parentally my head was not in the sand, it was under the sand! Guilty as charged!

Pondering my parental responsibility, I had to ask the hard questions. Had I ever told my sons not to disrespect a woman in this way or did I assume they already knew? Had I ever taught my daughter not to allow a boy to defile her publically or privately? Or, did I assume she knew? How much had I missed in terms of the reality that my children faced?

Had I witnessed this some time ago, I think my words and actions might have been clearer and different. We have talked with our children about sexuality but from a well manicured perspective, like sex after marriage. We taught them that every life has purpose and has value. Their job is to cause no harm to themselves or others so that purpose can be fulfilled. Certainly they should not allow others to pull them off course. We've even said, "Keep your peter in your pants," to the boys and "Keep your dress down" to the girls. I've joked and said, "Don't let a father come looking for you about his daughter. I will open the door and put you outside to deal with the consequences of your actions." I never thought I needed to discuss what to do while in high school. I presume I was hopeful that everything they learned at home and church would carry over to school.

Media imagery has certainly aided teenager's glorified view of sexual activity. One could easily cite movies, television programs, magazines, videos, electronic games, music videos and other types of media as contributors to the overplaying of sexuality. The burden is not theirs alone to bear. Media may have promoted sexuality, but our silence as parents, educator, churches and concerned citizens is viewed as consent.

There is no reservation about the fact that media in all forms flaunts sexuality. Sex is presented with such preponderance that the advertised product is often missed. Who can forget the Carl's Jr. Burger commercial with the young woman gyrating on an electronic rodeo machine while eating a burger? With real concerned parents and communities it would not have aired one day. The calls, letters, and emails would have shut it down. Since when should Victoria Secret capture prime time, family viewing hour? The answer is since schools, churches, parents, and communities have made no comment, nor logged complaints about the preponderance of sexuality in the media.

Cable Television along with its movie channels and uncensored programs create a whole new level of unbridled access to children. Since it is necessary in most areas to have a clear picture, cable has introduced R and X rated programming into our living rooms. This unprecedented access presents viewing opportunities that most parents are unaware of.

Times past required that individuals go to the theatre to see an R or X rated movie. Gratefully such rating restrictions prevented teen access. Programming of this nature now comes directly into the home. Promising only password protection, cable opens the floodgates to all that responsible parents would want to keep away from their children.

Cellular phones with internet access provide even more unbridled access to pornography and adult movies. Parents believe they are providing a communication tool; however, children gain access to damaging images all while the parent funds the access. Unfortunately, there are no restrictions on cellular phone access to internet sites.

The *Reality TV* craze also feeds into youthful sexuality. The name itself is such a misnomer. Offering no sound reasoning or concrete solutions to real life issues, it is gaining attention. Drama, freakish tasks, unbridled emotions, immature relationships and sex are the foundation of such programming. When is it normal, or ideal, for 25 women to compete for the affection of one man knowingly? Are there 25 men anywhere who will compete for the affections of one woman knowingly? I mean in real life, not because you are being paid to do so.

How often do real housewives gather to discuss their husbands, have lunch, shop incessantly and curse at each other? I do not know any. I am a wife who has cared for a home and family for over 25 years, I can assure you this is not reality.

Television programming, both censored and uncensored, cast people meeting for the first time, and within minutes having sex. Details for such scenes have moved from going into the bedroom and closing the door, leaving the imagination to the viewer, to undressed bodies, moving in unison. Instead of outrage from cable subscribers, we suffer in silence and some in ignorance, not knowing such programs exist and are piped into our homes daily.

Beyond the moral diversion from truth presented through television programming, parents have the sole responsibility to teach children that promiscuous, vile, and unscrupulous behavior is not good for real life or responsible television programming. Critical is their need to understand that most movies and reality programming are *NOT* real life. Life's issues are not settled in an hour or thirty minutes of taping.

How many parents send their children to school thinking that they will be leaning against a wall while a guy, or girl, is feeling over them? It never crossed my mind. When I think of school, classes, books, teachers, sports, shared lunches (where you swap off what you don't want from your lunch for somebody else's) crowd my thoughts. Visions of homework assignments, tests, reports and presentations all accompany school imagery. Exciting the loins and stirring up the libido in public are certainly not part of the framework I envisioned or experienced in high school.

The school system insisted that each student sign an acknowledgement of sexual harassment, yet no one was assigned to ensure that such activity did not happen on the campus. With that said, everyone was doing their assigned job. Teachers were ushering students in and out of the classrooms, security was making sure students were not fighting or hiding in restrooms. Whose job was it to maintain the integrity of the sexual harassment training or to maintain the personal integrity of the students? It sounds like a case for parent volunteers.

There are Consequences

In one class, an attractive, intelligent, well-poised student stood up to give a response to a question. I was saddened at the visual revelation that her life was about to change forever. I had seen her many times before, though she was always seated, now the reality of private activity was apparent. This well-spoken young lady was a pregnant teen with a typical stomach mass measuring about six-seven months. Though she was not counted in the 400,000+ teens in 2009, she was a visible statistic that day.

In hopes that my utter shock was not obvious, I smiled as her gaze met mine. In that smile was my heartfelt encouragement for her to continue with her future. In that smile was a "You can make it. Do not give up." Life would be more difficult with responsibility, but great possibilities existed ahead.

After class my son ran up to me and put his arm around my shoulder. He walked with me for the first time publically. He knew me all too well.

"You are sad, huh?" Josh inquired.

"Not really Son," I responded.

"It's because she's pregnant, right?" he confirmed.

"She can still have a great life. It will just be far more difficult," I shared.

"I know Mom. She is a good girl. She will be all right," he encouraged

"Thanks Son." I confirmed.

As he scurried off to catch up with his latest interest, I wondered if he really understood the meaning of difficulty. Teenagers do not count the cost of housing, utilities, formula, pampers, daycare, clothing, baby food, baby sitters and much more. Incalculable are the hours of lost sleep, the loss of freedom in this new lifetime commitment to another human being. Teenagers have no concept of real life so life often teaches them the hard way.

Several months after my tenure in high school ended, my son came home proud to present what he thought was good news.

"Mom, you remember the girl in my class that was pregnant?"

"Sure son. How is she? Did she have the baby?"

Not yet, but a few weeks ago she came to school and said her boyfriend proposed. He surprised her with a ring. She thought they were going out to dinner. Now they are married. They got married last weekend."

I sat on the steps and silently prayed. "Now what is the matter?" he asked.

"Honey she is so young to be married and having a child. I just hope all goes well with her."

"Mom, I know they are young. But at least he stepped up. Most guys get a girl pregnant and go on about their business. I don't know this guy, but I like him. He stepped up, Mom. He stepped up. You should respect the fact that he stepped up."

I smiled at the son I raised knowing there was so much I left out. So much I was unaware that he faced daily, so much I had failed to teach.

"You are right."

Then he hugged me as if to say, "Don't give up on my generation. We will do the best we know how. We will step up when needed. Don't give up on us Mom." And so to that end, *not giving up*, I write the next chapters of this book.

In consulting we are taught that if you are not part of the solution, you are part of the problem. Never wanting to be identified as a problem, finding viable solutions became the focus of my experience.

The Great Divide: The Educator and the Student

The results of a Public Agenda poll among educators illuminates the difference in expectation among students and teachers. While Generation Z clearly demonstrates the need to add supportive services to the education process the educators tend to see problem-free children as the desired audience. Rather than accept the changing complexity of the student body that occupies the seats of the smart classroom, the request for well-behaved children is atop the teacher wish list.

Rated more highly than strong administrative backing and support, when polled by Public Agenda, well-behaved students and parental support was favored by 83% of elementary and secondary school teachers. [35] Fifty-one percent of teachers thought unmotivated students would be a major drawback to teaching. Forty-one percent found behavioral problems as a major drawback to education. Thankfully, both disciplined students and parental involvement were preferred over a higher salary.

During the first year as a high school teacher, 64% believed they had *the difficult to reach students (Generation Z)*. While the study attributes difficult classrooms to a culturally diverse makeup, for purposes of this writing we liken a difficult classroom to be one that

---

[35] Gasbarra, Paul, "Public Agenda: Our Money, Our Schools: Top Ten Findings From our Research Team,"
< www.publicagenda.org/print/16983> (accessed August 2012).

contains 40-50% of students who fit the profile for Generation Z. Twenty three percent of teachers reported that they were not trained to work with an ethnically diverse group.

More than half of teachers, 52% found the training they received inadequate and of little value.[36] Eight percent (8%) found their training had no value at all. One might conclude that teachers do not feel adequately prepared to teach the difficult to reach students (Generation Z); therefore, their preference is to have a class of well-behaved or disciplined students with great parental support.

Contrast the teacher's desire for parental support with the shocking statement I received from a 20 year retired teacher. She remarked that I was the first parent she has seen in the classroom in 20 years. The visual is clearer. There is a continental shift between the teacher's desire for parental support and what they receive.

Comparing the statistics from Generation Z against the teacher's desire for a well- behaved classroom would conceivably reveal that almost half of the parents are unable to comply with discipline aspects due to their own challenges (drugs, alcohol, mental illness, homelessness, poverty, etc.). Compare and contrast the teacher's desire to have well-behaved, disciplined students with the statistics on children whose parents use drugs and alcohol, along with statistics on students who have been sexually abused or neglected. The resulting student behaviors are far from the teacher's desired conduct.

---

[36] Ibid

The perspective of principals and parents present an even greater divide. Seventy-nine percent of principals do not see the educational standards as an issue to education. Most believe students are not learning enough and the material is not difficult. While 65% of parents believe the students are learning more and the materials are harder than when they were students.

The hope of this writing is to provide children with the services and tools they need to become better students. When a child's basic needs are met, there is a greater likelihood of better behavior and better academic performance. Seeing that many necessary services are fragmented and separate from the educational setting, this manuscript proposes the joining of forces to meet the needs of the children. Motivating students to perform to high academic standards and behave accordingly can be realized after their basic needs are met.

Share-Worthy Experiences with Educators

While much time has been dedicated to Generation Z and all its nuances, it is critical to highlight the educators who not only understand their job, but understand the recipient of all they planned. My respect for the educator deepened. My prayers for them increased, and my hope is to aid their tenacity and commitment. Enjoy these firsthand encounters with Educators.

Economics Class

I thoroughly enjoyed economics class. I was sure the teacher enjoyed her subject matter and her students. Aside from the fact that I enjoy learning, I loved the atmosphere created by this particular teacher. From the moment you entered her room, you were acknowledged with a smile. If she was not seated at her desk, she was at the door ushering in her students. Wherever she was, she made a point to acknowledge each student by name.

Her preparation was obvious and appreciated. The teaching outline was on the board along with any homework assignment. She read it aloud and required that each student write it in their notebooks. She checked it and stamped their notebook. She gave notes regularly and students had to write them. She checked them also and they received a stamp. If the notes were not finished the stamps were not given. The stamps translated to points and points translated to increased grades. Much like the old S & H stamp book, at the end of collecting, there was a reward.

Her lesson plans included both current and historical events to expound economic principles. Products and businesses that the students were familiar with were researched to make the information more applicable to the young audience. She enlisted their buying practices and that of their parents to help clarify her points. Her lessons, by power point or overhead projector were not longer than 20 minutes. The rest was class activity, class discussion or independent practice. This was perfect timing and correct for their attention span.

After instruction and making sure notes were correct, the games began. Whether by rows or tables, students competed for extra credit points by answering the question correctly and shooting the Nerf basketball for two or three points. For the team who won, the extra credit points were given to each team member. The Nerf ball was then thrown around the room by the students to indicate who would answer the next question.

Amazingly every student participated before the class was over. The games were exciting. The competition was fierce. It was fun to see a team select a basketball player to take the shot and watch him/her miss, then see a girl who has never played basketball make the shot and become the team hero. Learning was fun and at its best. Even I enjoyed it.

The Economics teacher used creative games that appealed to both genders to enlist student participation. Students also came to the board to write their answers competitively. I noted most of the other teachers did not allow students to write on the board. It was reserved for their notes only. She found a way to use the board in a manner that was fun and increased learning. It also gave the students an opportunity to get up out of their seats.

The students also worked in teams and competed against each other in review. If the answer were correct and spelled properly the team won the extra points. Then I witnessed something remarkable.

The economics teacher openly admitted, that after the review game, she could tell that some lessons needed more instruction. I need to do a better job so that you will understand the information, she confessed. Her solution was to postpone the test, re-teach the lessons then reschedule the test. Hallelujah! The students drove the progress and not the completion of the lesson plan.

Here was a teacher who was focused on the needs of her audience. More than completion of the lesson, she wanted them to learn the contents. Through the review games, she determined that re-teaching was necessary. She had the courage to say so and to make adjustments for their learning. A common practice is to assign students to study more in certain areas to be successful on the test. However, when teaching is the job, teaching must be done until learning takes place. This she did masterfully. As a result, per her words, the class did very well on the test.

As a parent, I thoroughly appreciated the honest assessment of the need to re-teach. I respected the way she took responsibility without blaming the students for not studying or remembering. She said I need to do a better job. What a great lesson in personal maturity to teach her students. Realistically, she may have done a great job on the initial instruction; however, if her audience did not receive it, re-teaching was necessary.

The result of this style of teaching is that the students enjoyed Economics class, my child included. The students were all glad to come and participate. They even enjoyed doing the homework assignments. She prepared for them, and they in turn wanted to be prepared for her.

Not once did I hear sighing, complaining or rude outbursts about boredom in this class. No one screamed I don't get it! I even heard my child using economic terms outside of the class. That is every parents dream! Demonstrate what you are learning!

To my great surprise this hallmark for student inclusion and student driven learning tamed some of the seemingly untamable students from other classes. It was not until after my personal conversation with the Curser that I noticed he was in the same Economics class I attended for over six weeks. He clearly did not demonstrate the same behaviors as in Algebra II. He did nothing to draw attention to himself in this class prior to this moment.

The Economics teacher was complimenting the Curser on the number of signatures he had collected for an initiative he was taking to the State Senate. As she spoke, he looked in my direction. Our eyes met. I gave him a big smile and he nodded as if to say, I received it. He stood tall and walked proud as he shared the purpose of his trip.

The amazing thing is that he was in that class long before I spoke with him in Algebra II. He simply exhibited completely different behaviors in this class. He proved that when learning is fun, inclusive and student driven, you get a different atmosphere for learning and hence a more engaged student. What I find uncanny is that I did not notice him before that day. My seating was in the front of the class; however, I looked at each student on a regular basis. I do not know how I missed him but I was ecstatic to know he was doing better in other classes.

The Caring Teacher

Most teachers do their best to instruct; however, there are those who go beyond the call of duty to provide for students. We have heard stories of teachers providing extra school supplies for students in need and so much more. They deserve our gratitude and appreciation. Enjoy this delightful story of the Caring Teacher.

After securing permission to be on the school grounds so often, lunchtime presented a problem for me. I had no desire to sit with my child who sat with his interest at the time. A Caring Teacher, who knew of my tenure, invited me to come and have lunch in her room. She taught a college preparation course designed to help students select and apply to the colleges of their choice. She also gave up her Fridays and Saturdays to travel with them to visit college campuses. This was remarkable and not part of her pay structure.

I noticed during lunch her doorway was always crowded with students not assigned to her class that period. Eventually I learned why. She was the *free lunch lady*, if you will. She provided free peanut butter and jelly sandwiches at lunch for students who were hungry. She purchased the bread, peanut butter and jelly from her own money and simply served until it was gone. The students made their own sandwiches. She just put out the ingredients and monitored use to determine when to pull out more.

Interestingly enough, the students learned to share so that each person could have a sandwich. They made their own PB&Js and returned to their designated areas. Other teachers knowing what she provided sent their hungry students to be fed. She welcomed anyone. This went on at every visit. She also had a mini cabinet full of things to feed children.

Astounded, I asked why she did this. She responded with, "Most children skip breakfast because they are running late or there is no food. Others have no money for lunch and they are hungry. They need food to think. Peanut butter and jelly is relatively healthy for them. Many of them have practice after school and have eaten nothing all day. If I can help, I don't mind."

What a sacrifice? The beauty is that she saw a need and filled it. She embodied a concept that schools must embrace. Some children do not qualify for free lunch, but they are hungry. Some don't arrive in time to receive the free lunch they qualify for, but they are hungry. These are natural needs that must be met for students to perform. The great planners for our educational system could take a page from her book. If they are hungry, feed them.

One could imagine what type of financial strain this unfunded PB&J restaurant could have on one's income after an entire semester. I checked on the Caring Teacher's wellbeing periodically, even after my tenure ended. By Christmas time, the Caring Teacher decided to forego a Christmas tree for her own family. While the measure of her impact on hungry children was much greater than a single Christmas tree for a single family, she deserved the same quality of consideration and provisions. Through a longstanding business relationship with a Christmas tree provider, a beautiful Christmas tree was delivered to the Caring Teacher. Any parent who knew how much she provided for the children would have gladly helped. These details will be easily missed until parents really become the involved parents that teachers are hoping for. The Caring Teacher was humbled and honored to know that people cared enough to serve her as she had served so many.

Making New History – Working Together

I was pleasantly surprised when the history teacher put me to work in her class. Without forewarning, I became the teacher's aide. I presume that my face was familiar enough after six weeks or more, and I caused no interruptions. I was safe so I was put to work.

Kudos to the teacher who recognized I was not there for a performance. I was there for a greater purpose and could be a resource as needed. I have always appreciated a person who knew how to use their resources. For a short period, without a title or salary we made history. We worked together, parent and teacher.

I passed out papers. I collected papers. I turned on and off lights for her power point presentations. I answered the door, which locked automatically upon closing. I was asked to cover the back as she monitored the front during assignments. What a joy! Somebody finally put me to work. Somebody included me!

At the end of one class we held a brief conversation. She asked questions such as: What do you do? What brings you here so regularly since your son is doing well in my class? She shared that she admired my taking the time to come so regularly and she appreciated my willingness to help out. She ended her conversation by asking if I have any suggestions or comments that could help improve her class. She asked me to please share them with her. She said she wanted to learn more and do more for her students. She also admitted that she did not have all the answers.

It was a rare and awesome moment. How mature to admit not having all the answers, particularly when in your position answers are expected. I certainly understood what it meant not to have the answers. That is why I returned to high school. I appreciated her honesty and was more than willing to help. I just happened to have a few ideas.

We shared a few moments that were surprising to us both. I applauded her for seeing me as a resource and putting me to work. My recommendation was to regard her students as resources and put them to work as well. She really worked hard and it showed. She simply needed help and her able students were right there.

This teacher was well prepared every time I entered her class. I always learned something. Her teaching pace was great. In fact, she was so well prepared that nothing was required of the class but their attention. We talked about knowing your audience and using your resources as a means to allow student participation in the learning process.

Time spent in the classroom allowed me to become familiar with the habits of some of the students in her fourth period history class. I reminded her of the difficulty she had trying to correct basic student habits and behaviors. The recommendation was to study them and use them as an asset and a resource, rather than view them as a hindrance. It was a new perspective to see her students as the help she needed.

During class I looked for ways that she could liven up the classroom. She was a great teacher, in fact, so great the students were uninvolved. She announced that she had 32 pages left in the chapter before the chapter test. I happened to count her students and there were exactly 32 students. After her request for ways to improve her class, I suggested that she allow them to finish the chapter through a report and presentation. We flipped through the book and there were exactly enough subtitles for the students.

By the time I returned to the history class, presentations (3-5 minutes in length) had begun. Students presented their subjects through power point. The graphic designs were amazing. Some students creatively designed the words to their presentation to fly into position. Others chose to make major points blink to bring extra attention to them. Others went beyond the data in the book and added extra detail. This was a new class. It was no longer the group that screamed, *"I hate history. It's so boring!"* This was an involved class.

To add interest the teacher gave extra credit points to students who could answer questions about the presentations. The presenter had to ask three questions from their presentation. Those who answered got the extra credit points. Interestingly enough, students who did not usually pay attention were focused and they were excited about the opportunity to earn points.

There is more to being a participant in the learning process than meets the eye. It is the catalyst to something great. I was witnessing learning at its best. With the time allotted approximately 3-4 presentations were given in each class. Not only were the students receiving the information in snippets, but they could ask questions and compete for points. The students were also inadvertently learning presentation skills and how to speak in public as an added bonus. It was during this time that Trina Z transformed in the history class. She became a model student who increased the participation of those around her.

Interestingly enough, Baby Doll Z still requested the key to the restroom; however, her behavior was slightly modified. Baby Doll Z was now paying attention. She laughed when the others laughed. She smiled when someone did a good job. She was remotely involved via facial expressions and body language. In actuality, she did not participate but for the first time, she opened the bejeweled notebook and began to take notes.

There were no outbursts about boredom or hatred of the history class during student presentations. Every student who was previously perceived as a stumbling block to education was now in the role of the educator. They enjoyed it. I enjoyed watching them compete and guess for the extra points. It was amazing how much they retained from a five minute presentation. As for Baby Doll Z, there was simply a reserved focus, occasional smiles and a posture that said, "I am here today."

Order in the Court

Fifth period was the state standardized test class. Individuals who did not pass or had not taken the test due to school transfers were enrolled. The overall pressure for local schools to successfully complete this test was fueled by the possibility of state and government funding. On the individual level, a diploma at graduation was the just due reward for successfully completing the test. Otherwise, the student participated in graduation but received no diploma. The pressure to be successful, in my estimation, led to short cuts and some surprising activity.

The class was a mixture of sophomores, juniors and seniors. When I entered the class for the first time, the teacher was on the phone. My presence was a startling change in his routine. The look of surprise and panic seemed to set in. I took a seat in the back of the classroom near the computers. He must have missed the email or assumed I would not come to his class. He yelled from the front to ask if he could help me. I presumed I looked too old to be a student. I responded by saying I was a parent observer. Neither of us knew what that meant but it sounded official.

The best way to explain what I saw for the next 45 minutes was the wild kingdom. The teacher gave the instructions for the workbook and the students were allowed to get their own workbooks from the shelf. Unbridled freedom is the best way to describe this class. On the way to get the workbooks, there was friendly chatter, playful rough housing, jokes and lots of laughter. Paper was being thrown from one side to the other. Students were constantly changing seats and visiting their friends in class. There was much sharing of information and copying going on. It was a society without order.

I sat in total amazement at the lack of control. We needed order in the Court! The teacher seemed to be preoccupied at best. His focus was not his students and apparently had not been for some time because the students were quite comfortable with their behavior and saw nothing wrong with it. I, on the other hand was appalled. Now I knew why some of our students had difficulty passing the test. Who could learn in this environment?

The teacher sat at his desk and looked up occasionally but he saw nothing alarming. He once stated that the assignments in the workbook would help them pass the state test. Then I understood the difficulty. This was a class without instruction, at least that day. It was more like self help. It reminded me of the old SRA Reading Books in the back of the classroom when I was in elementary school. I often finished my work quickly to go on the self guided tour through literature. The major differences were that my class was orderly, the work did not affect my grade, nor did my diploma rest on how many books I completed. This was too important to be self guided.

During the class, the date of the next scheduled state test was given. The students had three weeks to prepare before it would be administered again. I was certain my student had difficulty learning in this environment. The lack of order in the class prompted me to wait to speak to the teacher after class.

After greeting the teacher, I thanked him for allowing me to observe. I asked if I could have a workbook to take home for study. He said I could not have a book and responded as though he was offended that I asked for one. He said I would need permission from the Principal to take a book home. I thanked him for his time and departed.

My First Visit to the Principal's Office

Shortly after the discussion with the state exam teacher, I headed to the Principals office to get the much needed permission for the workbook. The Principal asked how I ended up in the class and I explained. She was intrigued and appreciative of my presence on campus. Then I requested permission to use a workbook for the state test exam. I explained that there were only three weeks left and I believed my student might benefit from a quieter environment.

She asked me to expound on my comment. I got a little choked up and told her I might be able to explain more at a later date. I did suggest that she monitor and even attend the state testing class and see what she thought. In the meantime I asked that she trust me with one workbook which I promised to return. I was able to clear my voice enough to say that Economics class was great and the English class was good.

As we departed her office, the state exam teacher appeared in the hallway. His face looked like he saw a ghost when the Principal and I appeared together. She politely asked him to give me a book. He graciously provided one and I thanked him.

The next week, change was in the air in the state exam class. The teacher assigned seats (this late in the school year) and insisted that the students stay in them. He taught a mini lesson, worked examples on the board with the students and then assigned them to the workbook. He presented a lesson on the overhead projector and required that they take notes. This was a first, I heard from the students.

What a respectable and much appreciated change! I could only assume that the Principal observed the class. Whatever caused the change, I appreciated it. I learned some intriguing things about the state exam. After a few sessions, I began to enjoy the class. As time drew nearer for the test to be taken, I developed a new concern.

The week before the exam, the teacher spent the entire class time teaching about the probability of test answers. He taught them that with a 100 question, multiple-choice test, probabilities existed for the correct answers. He proceeded to teach that with the choice of A, B or C selections, if they answered A to every question, they would be correct 33% of time. If they answered B for every answer, they would be correct 33% of the time and likewise with letter C. He stated that if they did not know anything, this method would allow them at least 33% on the test.

As a parent, I was disappointed and appalled. Who does that? Who circles all A's on a test hoping for 33%? Why was the educator teaching the children a method that completely bypassed what he taught the entire semester? Where was the educator's confidence in what he had taught, or in what the students had learned?

As soon as the class was over I caught up with my son and said, "Erase everything he just said. Don't you ever go into any test and simply circle answers. You had better read every question and give it your best evaluation before you answer."

"Okay Mom! Why are you mad at me? I would not do that! Calm down," he said defensively.

He was right. He did not teach this mess. I just wanted to make sure he never followed it. So I replied, "I am sorry that you had a teacher who taught students a horrible short cut to failure. Son, there are some things you just cannot do."

This just so happened to be the class where I uncovered the cheating network. Now I understand how it could exist. When educators have little to no confidence in their student's ability to learn, the student seeps to their low level expectations. Contrarily, if an educator has confidence in their students and openly shares that confidence and high expectation, the student will rise to the standard.

In a quieter environment I required my student to review the workbook on his own to prepare for the state testing. Several weeks later the principal called him to the office to personally inform him that he passed the test. Per his description, she was as excited as he was. I appreciated the personal touch. It also confirmed that she witnessed the before and after atmosphere of the state testing class and saw the need for change.

I appreciated the principal's prompt response to my recommendation to audit the state testing class. The resulting changes benefitted the entire student body. Her input helped restore the atmosphere for learning which is critical to the success of all students.

The English Teacher

Observing English was a new experience for me. It had become the technological bridge to education with each student capturing their thoughts, writings and assignments on laptop computers. All writing had to be done in class and on the laptop computer. The student's work was saved to a flash drive which they brought to class each day.

I understood the reasoning to capture all writing in class. The purpose was to help insure authenticity. In reality, writing has much to do with mood, atmosphere and motivation. Call me old fashioned but I missed the concept of pen to paper with the goal of typing it later. Nonetheless, these were seniors in high school. The assignments were relevant and students wrote about life experiences, life goals and aspirations. This particular teacher wanted her students to know what it would take to reach their goals from an educational, financial and administrative standpoint. While it was all relative and in time, I thought it lacked instruction and screamed for guidance.

While the students were assigned to work quietly, I assumed the task of observation. I noted that many students clandestinely pulled out their cell phones to text, check emails and check messages. I thought the cell phone in the classroom was a major distraction to education and my gaze was no deterrent to this technological interruption. With that said, I am sure there were policies in place stating that cell phones should not be visible in class.

When the lesson plan is omitted and anchors for independent practice such as review are bypassed, distractions easily flow into the class environment. I am uncertain how much work was accomplished by each student. What I can say is that the senior project was a large undertaking that included many steps for completion. I was privileged enough to observe the end product and it was great.

This teacher had a vision and the end product proved to be valuable. In the process of reaching that goal, the day to day classroom dynamics suffered. My presence did not hinder or alter her process. Mostly I sat in silence while she worked. Rarely was a question asked of her. The experience was somewhat uneventful. While I had hoped to witness her teaching, I missed that opportunity. However, the end goal was met. Her students appeared to be successful.

Personal Call to Duty

My son observed some of my conversations and inquired as to why I was talking to "strangers." I found it interesting that he labeled his classmates as strangers. He was particularly interested in what I said to the Curser. Unless he reads this book, he will not know. Although it was heartwarming to know that he cared, I recorded the overall lack of correct community among the youth. They had formed a sense of community strong enough to copy from one another but not one strong enough to study together and prohibit cheating from one another (the correct approach to academic challenges). Where they learned to compromise on such an important character issue has yet to be determined.

After considering my own limitations, I reminded him that every man has a *Call to Duty* to his/her own education. All students must apply themselves to the task of being successful. I looked at him squarely in the eyes and said, "My purpose for being here has expanded. It started with you, but it's bigger than you or I alone. It involves you but the experiences I have had are not just for you and me. I have no idea what to do with all that I have learned here, but I have to do something. Now that I know that what you said to me about your classes is true, I now challenge you to the call of duty to your own education, son."

He looked at me and said, "Will you trust me to solve my algebra II problem without you? You know I am already going to graduate so let me solve my Algebra problem." I stared at him with piercing eyes. He did not flinch, blink or grin. He was serious.

I understood the real meaning of his question. A year ago he changed his class schedule and it upset the entire order of the household. We came and went as a group but every child attended a different school. His change affected us all and we scrambled to make it work. We emphatically told him to consult us before he made any changes that would affect the rest of our schedules.

I fully understood it was his problem to solve. We tried a tutor who worked well with our son. At the most critical time he began having health challenges. I tried coming to school myself and I could not understand the material. Having done all I knew to do, I relinquished Algebra II. Finally I said, "I trust your judgment."

What this teenager was able to achieve in a few days astounded me. He went to the office to find out who was the math department chairperson. He scheduled a meeting and pointedly asked the department chair, "Who is the best person to teach me Algebra II? Who is the best we've got?"

He was given a name. He went to see that teacher and discussed his issues. He learned that the best person to teach had been assigned to geometry and algebra I only that year. My student went back to the math department chairman and explained what happened with the first choice. He then asked, "Who is the second best person to teach me?" He was given another name. He requested permission to sit in that teacher's class for one day. He received the pass and sat in the back until he finished.

He informed the recommended teacher that the math department chairman thought he was the best person to teach him algebra II. He went on to ask if he would squeeze him in one of his classes. He was willing to stand if needed to and would rearrange his entire schedule to be successful in algebra II. The teacher was impressed with his commitment toward his own education and agreed to help him.

By the time I returned for my next visit, his schedule was completely changed. He reminded me that I trusted his judgment and confirmed that he was sure he made the right decisions.

I stopped at the counselor's office and received the new schedule. She commented on how well he was doing. She appreciated the responsibility he was taking for his own education.

I felt like I had started high school all over again as I sat in the back of the new algebra II class. I did not know this group. There was no Curser among them. Not a single student requested my help during my few visits. In fact, what I witnessed was quite remarkable. It was education at its best.

It was student driven. This appeared to be a much larger class with approximately 40 students. The teacher confirmed that he did his best to make room for whoever needed his help. The change was certainly a different style of teaching with a completely different atmosphere for learning. The teacher had control over the classroom, not resulting from belittling comments but respectful concern over their wellbeing. His teaching style was student driven, student inclusive and smooth.

I call him Mr. Smooth. His methods for solving equations were quite clear. I could write them down and remember them. The examples were pertinent to class work and homework. His methods were simply a different and clearer way of solving problems. He did not use two white boards even though he covered the same material. He used one sheet of transparency paper.

Every student in the class was taking notes from the overhead. He engaged his students and asked questions. They helped him with each step. He wrote what they said, only if it were correct. He asked the right questions to get the right answers. He reminded students of previously taught information. Most importantly, my student could follow this method of solving algorithms.

The students were focused and attentive even though there were forty students in his class. He received special permission from the Math Department Chairperson to include my son. He respected the fact that the student sought help and asked for the best. Therefore, he made an exception to allow him in that class.

My student was a changed young man after this new schedule was confirmed. His quiz and test scores improved drastically. He gladly reported what he made on a quiz or test. This was in stark contrast to his actions before in Mr. Einstein's class. We practically had to wait until the mid quarter grades or parent portal was updated to know his standing. From my few notes taken in class, I could offer help if needed. However, he no longer required it. "I understand now," was his response.

I could not have been more proud of my son for seeking better for himself. He accepted the *call to duty* for his own education. I was pleased with the results. I also felt better about my own brain's ability to recollect and learn Algebra II. I could actually follow the new teacher. I understood what he was teaching and how he taught it. His teaching pace was learner friendly and ultimately profitable for the young and mature mind.

I remembered how I felt trying to keep up with Mr. Einstein. I compared it to the joy I had learning from Mr. Smooth. There was no comparison. I felt dumb each time I left Mr. Einstein's class. I questioned my own ability to learn as I am certain many students did as well. This was a welcomed relief; one that I appreciated for my son and myself. However, I had a deep concern for all the students we left struggling in Mr. Einstein's class. I wondered how we could change their outcome in Algebra II like Mr. Smooth had changed my son's.

Recognizing that my options were limited in terms of solving the issues for every student in Mr. Einstein's class, I committed it to prayer. The desire to see every student leave the classroom with the confidence to master the information was my goal, how to achieve it was my new concern. At that moment I considered myself an involved parent. An involved parent is one who has progressed from simply wanting better for their child to wanting what is best for all children. *Yes, I am an involved parent.*

A Message to All Students… Know Your Role

While it is our hope to have successfully communicated the plight of several high school students, it is also our goal to prepare students for education as well. Two things were stressed at home to our children to keep them in a teachable position. First: Know your role. You are the student. Your role is to respect the teacher and follow instructions. Your opinion is important to you and to us simply because we are your parents. When asked, you may respectfully give a response. Participate in every opportunity to learn. Otherwise you should be a delight to have in class.

As a result of rule #1 our eldest son was known as the "Mayor" at his private, all male high school. During parent teacher conferences I was always told he was a *delight to have in class* and that he always knew what to say and what not to say. When I introduced myself to one teacher, he recognized the last name and said, "*So you are the mother of the Mayor.*" In surprise I responded, "Excuse me." He responded by giving my son's real name and said, "Oh, yeah, he is the Mayor around here. He always knows exactly what to say. He knows how to talk up and how to talk down. If he were a politician, I would vote for him." He followed up by saying, "You should be proud. He is a good kid. We love him around here."

I stood in utter shock. Who is this mayor? Do I know him? I would like to meet him and receive those same perfect responses at home. I went home and told my husband, "We have given birth to a Mayor." Nonetheless, I was proud that he learned to show respect and as a result, he was respected. To date, when he comes home from college and visits his old school, the administrators and teachers still remember him. It amazes him that he left an indelible impression. It pleases us as parents as well.

Our second school rule: Make your education personality proof. You might really like a class or you may find a class boring. You may love the teacher or you may not like the teacher. The teacher may think you are great or not so great. These are all natural human reactions and they do happen. However, neither one should alter your success in the classroom. It is true that personalities do not always mix well. As the student, make sure that you are not at fault as a result of disrespect or mismanagement of your academic affairs.

Every student must know his job as a student is to, *"Get what you came for and don't leave until you get it."* Every student must know their responsibility to get the education, gain the knowledge, and retain it for the good of his life. Most importantly, do not allow the actions of others to cause you to lose focus of your goal.

We made it clear that information does not always come the way you want to receive it. The opportunity to learn is not always presented in a fun or interesting manner, but learn you must. Teachers, instructors and college professors will not always teach in the most exciting and inclusive way; however, this does not change your role. Your responsibility to your education must be stronger than any lack that you encounter in their presentation.

Our daughter struggled with pre-calculus. To overcome her challenge she persuaded two other students to meet her in the teacher's room at lunch. It was his break time and he allowed them to come and work out problems on the board during his break. He called her the hardest working student he had ever taught. Had I missed parent-teacher conference, I would not have learned of her extra effort to succeed.

Unbeknown to most teachers is that their perceived impression of a student's ability to learn and the environment they foster for learning are critical to the development of any individual. As a student, your level of preparation, attention to detail and willingness to apply yourself to your own success can dispel many preconceived notions.

There may be times when a request to change a class is necessary for your success. Remember it is for your success. Be willing to labor for your success. At no time should 98% of any class fail or even 20%. Should that be the case, it is time to involve administration. Your goal is not to place blame or find fault but to find ways to be successful within your school system. Exercise your *call to duty* and make it happen.

Should you find that the issues that plague Generation Z are present in your own life, do not suffer in silence. Find a trustworthy adult within the school system and unload your burden. Remember that you are never the only one who suffers with whatever your problem may be. There is support for you. However, you must seek it. It is our hope at the end of this manuscript to include much needed resources as integral components of education.

Continue to press toward your goals regardless of obstacles. Obstacles are opportunities in disguise. Find the opportunity and allow it to help you grow and develop. Whatever you do, don't quit on your education or this phase of your life. There is so much more ahead for you. Your latter will be greater; however, you must continue to press forward to reach the goal.

Education: A Broader Scope

The statistical overview of Generation Z simply exposed the complexity of our classroom makeup and confirmed that the occupants of the smart classroom are quite different than the common perception of students. Therefore, our preparation must be adjusted to meet their needs. Currently, 40-50% of the students in our schools are not represented in the learning process because their needs are greater than the current scope of education.

Our educational practices and methods are much the same as they were almost half a century ago when I attended school. The practices that are successful should be applauded. However, others simply need an adjustment or an adjunct to make them more effective. The task to educate must be expanded when the needs are greater than the scope. Rather than lose the student our system might be broadened to encompass all that a student would need to be successful. The following comprehensive educational plan proposes solutions for our challenged system of education.

A Comprehensive Educational Plan

While traditional education includes tools necessary for reading, writing and arithmetic, the purpose of this writing is to introduce as well as recommend a broader scope to our endeavors. The goal is to meet the uncharted needs of the populace within our borders. This comprehensive educational plan certainly agrees that traditional education must remain; however, it must increase its ability to identify and serve the full populace.

Conceding that our education system is the only entity in our culture that maintains a legal right to a minimum of eight hours of a student's day for almost ten months each year, it is the best arena in which to expand our scope. Other than home, there is no other system that legally monopolizes the time of our children; therefore, expanded services would best be offered from this arena. Besides the home, it is also the only system that can combine the value of nutritional reform, physical health reform and consort with social and behavioral agencies to meet the needs of students. Generation Z has clearly demonstrated in both behavioral and academic outcomes that more than traditional education is necessary for successful outcomes.

This manuscript proposes a *four-phased* approach to education that will serve the entire trinity of man – the mind, body and soul. The four phases are Nutrition, Academic, Physical and Psychosocial services (**NAPP** Program). Study the following diagram.

Nutrition Academics Physical Psychosocial (NAPP) Program

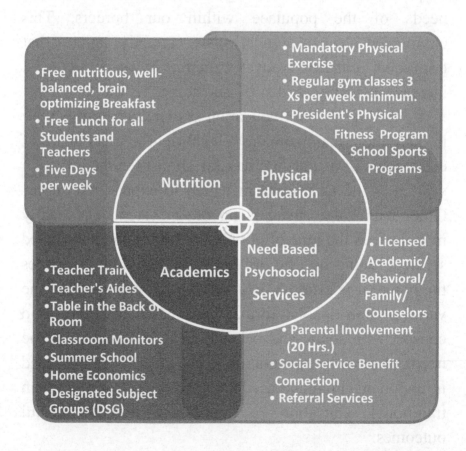

Deferring to the Hierarchy

Abraham Maslow created a theory commonly referred to as a *Hierarchy of Needs*. Though created to help establish a foundation for motivation in the workplace, it is equally beneficial to the educational paradigm simply because the *job of all students is to work on their education*. Teachers *teach* and students *work* to attain an education worthy of their life goals and aspirations.

In light of Maslow's theory that lower level needs must be met before higher level needs are endeavored, as well as the statistics revealed with *Generation Z – Statistically Speaking,* our educational platform must be expanded to meet the needs of all its constituents including the 40-50% that have needs greater than that of basic education. The concept of meeting the needs of the whole student could drastically change the current educational system as we know it. Our nation must expand the borders of education to include meeting the needs of the mind, body and soul and we will see greater possibilities for successful outcomes. Thus far, our focus appears to have been solely on the mind, evidenced by the less than favorable outcome of limited physical education.

A new perspective is offered herein to meet the most basic biological and physiological needs of the student population by providing the essential needs that are critical factors to student success. The provisions and maintenance for the NAPP program would be contained within the educational system. Ultimately our current system would broaden its purpose and influence in relation to a child's overall well-being.

The importance of a well balanced nutritious breakfast for proper brain functioning has been well documented. A preponderance of research has been published on the subject. Researchers have also confirmed the negative effects of skipping breakfast on the academic performance of children.[37] Yet many school children leave home without breakfast or ingest a substandard breakfast of high fat and high sugar foods, two enemies to good brain function. Low test scores, inability to concentrate and poor performance are directly linked to a poor breakfast or skipping breakfast.

Lunch is another important meal of the day, yet many students consume fast foods or prepackaged foods loaded with salt, chemicals and high fat. These factors are major contributors to obesity and illnesses such as diabetes and high blood pressure in children. If our educational platform were expanded to include the nutritional aspect for two very important meals of the day, behavior, attention span, focus and overall health could drastically improve.

---

[37] Action for Healthy Kids: Fact Sheet,
<http://sboh.wa.gov/Meetings/2003/10_15/documents/pmTab08-Factsheet.pdf> (accessed April 2013).

Obesity is an underlying factor and major contributor to heart disease, diabetes and stroke. The *2012 Statistical Fact Sheet* for the American Heart Association and American Stroke Association indicates that one in three children between ages 2-19 are overweight and obese. One in six children is obese in America.[38] It is estimated that the cost of obesity will be 254 billion dollars (includes medical cost and loss of productivity). To thwart these inevitable projections, a small portion of this amount could be used to invest in our student's health. Simply providing the proper food for our children twice a day, our nation could save them from a chronic illness and ultimately save their lives. By comparison and future projection, it is one of the smartest investments we could make in our educational system.

---

[38] American Heart Association, American Stroke Association, "Statistical Fact Sheet 2012 Update – Overweight and Obesity," <http://www.heart.org/idc/groups/heart-public/@wcm/@sop/@smd/documents/downloadable/ucm_319588.pdf> (accessed May 2012).

Nutrition Academics Physical Psychosocial (NAPP) Program

Nutrition

Nutrition is the first phase of the NAPP program. It is an integral part of the education process and no longer seen as separate or provisional to low income families only. As part of the NAPP educational program, meals are free and available to students and teachers alike. The nutritional well being of our educators is encompassed in NAPP so that they, too, can perform at optimal levels for our children.

Including a nutritious breakfast and lunch for all students and faculty would essentially dismiss the effects of poor food choices on academic performance. Offering only healthy nutritious foods, provided free of charge to students and faculty allows the system to control student's intake at least during the school day. With food offerings planned for optimal brain function, our students and faculty would be able to function at optimal levels.

The scope of education would be broadened to include nutritious meals twice a day for our children and teachers. While we often speak of poor nutrition in reference to children, some adults have poor eating habits as well. Accepting the responsibility for the nutrition of both parties could yield generational benefits with both short term and long term outcomes.

Establishing a comprehensive nutrition program for our schools would:

- ❖ Alleviate the negative effects of poor food choices on the brain which affects both the behavioral and cognitive functions. High sugar and high fat, the hallmark ingredients of convenient, ready to go foods, are common in breakfasts choices among students. The effects of sugar, fat, salt and dyes in food can cause an inability to focus, excitability – or hyperactive behaviors. (Academic Impact/Behavioral Impact)
- ❖ Set a pattern for healthy eating five days a week, for ten meals a week, thereby waging an effective war against childhood obesity. Ultimately, it would affect the overall health of our nation for generations to come. (Health/Economic/Behavioral Impact)
- ❖ Improve the quality of health for our students and expose them to the value of healthy food consumption. The ultimate hope is that exposure to healthy living will change their behavior at school, home and in the community. (Quality of life/Healthy Lifestyle/Social Impact)
- ❖ Meet the needs of students whose families are unable to provide a nutritious breakfast or lunch who may never qualify for a free lunch but the children are hungry nonetheless. (Social Impact)

- Destroy the status barrier between those students who can afford to buy lunch versus those who cannot. (Social Impact)
- Increase employment by staffing our school cafeterias with full time employees that prepare fresh meals daily and adds skilled workers to the workforce. (Economic Impact)
- Increase our investment in school culinary programs necessary to reverse the unhealthy trends of fast food consumption. (Educational Impact)

If our nation would count the cost of poor academic performance on our educational system and poor health outcomes due to obesity and diseases resulting from improper nutrition, it would realize that this program could be easily afforded. Future projections indicate that we cannot afford to omit proper nutrition in our schools. The benefits of reaching generations by setting this national standard for proper nutrition will far outweigh the investment.

By broadening our scope to include free nutritious meals daily, children are provided the most basic human needs. Students no longer have to be concerned about whether there is food at home for breakfast or lunch. With NAPP all children are provided for equally.

How to implement the Nutrition phase of the NAPP Program

Each state would employ the services of certified nutritionists to plan ten monthly menus of nutritious meals for breakfast and lunch. Meals should include the proper portions of proteins, fruits and vegetables with minimal carbohydrates from whole wheat and multi-grains. Menus should include fresh seasonal produce. Whenever possible, all foods provided should be cooked on-site with wholesome ingredients to avoid excess salt, sugar, fat and additives. Meals should *not* be prepackaged, pre-cooked or preserved.

To encourage exchange of ideas and creation of new possibilities for menu plan options, each state could post their initial ten month menus. After the initial submission of menus, the wealth of data from each state would provide enough healthy menus for years to come. Each day's menu should include two to three food options so that students can make wholesome choices. For example, breakfast could be the following options: oatmeal with raisins, turkey bacon, whole grain cold cereal (w/soy, rice or almond milk), fresh fruits, eggs (boiled or scrambled), whole grain toast, vegetable omelet, buckwheat pancakes, applesauce, orange juice, fruit smoothies and apple juice. Whatever the student selects as his/her food choice will be wholesome and will aid brain functioning.

The Nutrition program for our nation's schools should be federally funded. Federal funding would provide for the nutrition of our children as a national initiative. Due to the overall health and economic benefits from long term nutrition, the cost of the program is affordable. Ultimately, our medical costs will decrease and employment rates will go up. Most importantly, we will have taken responsibility for our nation's children as an investment in our future.

Children who are on special diets or have food allergies will be able to *opt out* of the free meals or to select from those items that meet their needs. The purpose of wholesome meals prepared on site is to avoid many of the food allergies caused by additives. Special attention will be given to provide gluten-free, nut-free, dairy-free options for all students. Our commitment to proper nutrition will aid the learning process and the benefits will be seen in the classroom.

What benefit would the nutrition program have in our classrooms? Per Abraham Maslow, Theory of Motivation, one of the most basic human needs will be met within the educational scope of responsibility. A proper nutrition program removes both the psychological and sociological effects of hunger seen in children. Conceivably, it would also eliminate the ill effects of a high-sugar, high- fat, high-salt, and additive-rich diet for both the student and the teacher. Ultimately, student achievement and behaviors would improve as a result of a well-balanced diet. Teacher productivity would increase and their overall disposition would improve because their basic need is met as well. Our teachers and children are worth the investment.

How will breakfast affect our school schedule?

Each school will have to begin its day 30-45 minutes earlier to accommodate breakfast for all students and faculty. The logistics would have to be addressed at each institution to accommodate all students. Opportunities to teach good table etiquette, good manners, the proper way to chew and digest food, and proper posture for digestion exists during meal times. The overall benefits would be well worth any addition or shift in time.

A Case for Home Economics

The Nutrition segment of this program has been highlighted for the health benefits it would afford our children. The resulting Culinary Arts Program was originally proposed as an optional class for students. However, history would make a great case for the resurgence of the now obsolete Home Economics program. The Home Economics program was once a graduation requirement for all females. With the goal of teaching basic life skills such as nutrition, components of well balanced meals, safe food handling practices, budgeting for food cost, some childcare, actual cooking, and actual sewing, this class singularly taught young women how to manage a household and a family. Both men and women continue to have households and families yet the ability to manage them properly has been compromised by lack of knowledge. Both genders would benefit from what this class teaches.

In the absence of Home Economics, fewer men and women know how to budget, how to plan a nutritious meal, and even fewer know how to cook or sew. The inability to properly care for infants, toddlers and young children is revealed in the prevalence of emergency room visits, child abuse, obesity and more. Parents are failing to teach their children basic nutrition, basic food preparation, and cooking because they did not learn how to do such things themselves. Boston Children's Pediatric Hospital is making a case for the return of Home

Economic citing the alarming obesity rate as a viable cause.[39]   Bloggers and websites flood the internet supporting the resurgence of Home Economics in the public school system. While the public may find it necessary, not only has it been removed as a graduation requirement, very few schools include it as a course offering.

The Nutrition segment of the NAPP program would easily allow integration of the timeless and necessary components of Home Economics for the betterment of our families. It could conceivably be part of the Culinary Arts Program extending the timeline to one year rather than one semester as offered in times past.

[39] Jeltsen, Melissa, *Bringing Back Home Economics,*
<http://childrenshospitalblog.org/bringing-back-home-economics/> (accessed May 2012).

Nutrition Academics Physical Psychosocial (NAPP) Program

Academics

The scope of academics in the NAPP program is broadened from student centered education only to include extensive teacher training. Equal to being certified to teach in a specific subject area is the need to be appropriately trained to teach the multifaceted audiences one might encounter. Teacher training will include segments to help teachers:

- ❖ Properly Identify their Audience (Multiple Intelligences)
- ❖ Make Education Interactive and Participative (Resource Utilization)
- ❖ Meet the Needs of their Audience
- ❖ Properly Handle Disciplinary Actions Supplement the Lessons with Learning Tools (Kahn University is one of many excellent resources)
- ❖ Recognize Signs of Abuse, Maltreatment, etc. and make necessary referrals for students
- ❖ Provide a Mandatory Teacher's Aide for each class
- ❖ Provide a *Table in the Back* of the room for student who require more help
- ❖ Work effectively with Parent Volunteers
- ❖ Develop and utilize the Designated Subject Groups (DSG's)

Know Your Audience

During our teacher training many years ago, the instructor drilled into us, "know your audience." While I am unsure of what the current contents of teacher training entails, certainly this component should not be overlooked. Knowing your audience includes, but is not limited to, knowing your support and your opposition. In particular, the teacher must know what happens in the lives of youth that support the educational process and what hinders the educational process. Proper application of such vital information allows the teacher to use viable options to encourage the activities that support education and challenge the hindrances.

Have you ever witnessed a young person play electronic games like X-Box 360's, Game Boys, PlayStations and similar products? It is simply marveling. The speed at which they create their own players, build their teams, and then compete can leave one awestruck. Interactive games such as the Wii and PlayStation offer components where the individual is actively involved and their body movements and actions are recorded and become part of the "live" game experience.

The makers of PlayStation and the Wii (trademark name) have studied their youthful audience and know the value of interactivity play. It would behoove our educators to take a page from their research and apply it. Sales clearly indicate that interaction is the hallmark of game play. Parents agree because they purchase these products and deliver them to their children as entertainment. This interactive entertainment is having a direct effect on the dynamics in the classroom.

Much of America's pastimes involve electronic media or media play. Researchers estimate that 80% of Americans (190 million households) will connect their video game consoles to the internet in 2012 and the percentage of households that play computer/video games is 65%.[40] *Child Health Data* reports that almost 40% of children play more than one hour, but less than four hours of video games or watch television daily. An additional 11% spend four or more hours on games or television daily.[41]

Playing video games creates stimulation that is associated with dopamine, a chemical produced by the brain. Dopamine produces feelings of excitement, joy, pleasure and pain. It is also a major contributor to physical movement and cognitive functioning. A UK researcher likened playing video games to snorting a line of cocaine, whose drug properties are often used to treat brains deficient in dopamine production. Teens find video games exciting, stimulating and, by the very nature of

---

[40] Video Game Statistics Industry Figures and Information, "Video Game Industry Stats," <http://www.grabstats.com/statcategorymainaspc?statCatID=13 > (accessed September 2012).

[41] National Survey of Children's Health – 2007, "Time Spent Watching TV or Playing Video Games," <http://childhealthdata.org/browse/survey/resultls?q=283&r+1> (accessed April 2012).

games, participative. Playing video games is like taking a drug that excites them, gives them pleasure and allows them to participate. This overall pleasurable effect experienced with dopamine production makes it difficult to keep children from engaging in gaming activity.

Unfortunately, some have taken video gaming to the extreme. Such actions have resulted in loss of lives and hospitalization and damage to specific areas of the brain. Fox News reported the health risks related to teen deaths caused by relentless video gaming.[42] Blood clots from long sedentary positions, dehydration and vein thrombosis are highly probable with long term gaming. Use of magnetic resonance imaging (MRI) revealed that specific areas of the brain that control cognitive function and emotional control were affected after 10 hours of "*shoot 'em up*" video games.[43] After one week without video games, the brain began to improve.

Highly interactive games cause a high level of stimulus to the brain. Over prolonged periods of stimulation, the brain becomes accustomed to a high degree of excitement. This same over-stimulated brain enters the classroom in the body of a preteen or teenager. Contrariwise, the educator is tooled with a bulletin board,

---

[42] Oskin, Becky. Fox News, "Teen and Video Games: How Much is too Much?" August 13, 2012, <http://www.foxnews.com/health/2012/08/13/teens-and-video-games-how-much-is-too-much/#ixzz278sTlOHn> (accessed September 2012).

[43] Waugh, Rob, Daily Mail. co.uk., "Violent Games Do Alter Your Brain," <http://www.dailymail.co.uk/sciencetech/article-2067607/Violent-games-DO-alter-brain--effect-visible-MRI-scans-just-_week.html#ixzz2797eHRqY> (accessed September 2012).

chalk, paper, a book and possibly an overhead projector for a power point presentation. This over-stimulated brain is asked to sit and quietly listen or take notes as the teacher speaks for 45-50 minutes, with the possibility of questions being answered at the end of the lecture.

What then is the over stimulated brain's assessment of education after electronic play? BORING! BORING! BORING! Why? At home these students have built virtual championship teams, won the playoffs, competed in the Super Bowl. They are winners of the NBA and NFL Championships. They have won Wimbledon, the World Cup, the World Series and the Masters. Now they are sitting in classrooms from 7:30AM to 3:30PM waiting for something exciting to happen. They wear a green jacket at home on video and hold up the coveted trophy; but at school, they are asked to sit and be quiet. Their brains now crave involvement, excitement and stimulation. As educators, it is our responsibility to know our audience and to find ways to make them an active part of the educational process.

Knowing your audience is a major component to an enjoyable and interactive learning environment. With 65% of all households using electronic games, a considerable number of students have over stimulated brains when they reach the school grounds. Feeding the frenzy daily is the interactive game play in applications on their cell phones and IPADs, etc. All of which, in comparison, renders the classrooms *boring* in the eyes of the beholder. Educators must rise to the challenge and properly serve our audience. This level of "pertinent" information goes beyond the feelings of the provider. When charged to educate, educate one must; however, as the audience changes, so must our methods to reach that audience.

Exactly what message should be given to our educators? In short, your audience has changed, so must your teaching methods and style. One might argue that education is not a game and parents must teach their children to set the proper expectations of the different environments. Parents could do exactly that; however, an over-stimulated brain is in the midst. Once stimulated, it seeks more stimulation. The question is, "Can the student find a high level of stimulation in the classroom?" Traditionally, the answer would be "no"; however, the possibilities are endless even without technology or electronics in the classroom environment.

A good education is priceless; it is clearly not a game. Education is a necessary, life-changing and critical component to success. It is also greatly affected by what the audience brings to the learning environment. Technology's play has introduced an environment that is fueled by excitement and entertainment. That same environment must be used to transform the classroom and make each child a winner. Exactly what does this mean?

Learning should be exciting and enjoyable! Can you remember the last time you learned something and enjoyed it? Did you participate in the process? Was there a question to which you sought the answer or an interest that provoked your desire to learn? You became involved in the process to seek the information you desired. For that reason, you remember most of what you learned. You were an active participant in your learning process.

To initiate learning, one must involve the learner. In short, learning must be interactive to maintain the attention span of the audience and to extract the best that each student has to offer. Gone (or should be) are the days where the teacher talks for 50 minutes and the students simply listen. The educator must find ways to integrate each student's strengths and weaknesses into the learning environment without the use of technology, but with a high-level integration of the mind and body. Students have a relentless and uncanny ability to let you know who they are and to expose the untapped abilities they possess. When teachers recognize these abilities, it is critically important to use them to complement the learning environment. The following examples will seem so simple, you might reject them. From experience, I can assure you, they work.

Identifying Your Resources

In every classroom, there will be students who talk without permission, leave their seats and walk within the classroom without permission, hum or sing. Observe long enough and you will find doodlers; you will find those who are quiet and attentive along with those who spontaneously work in groups. Almost invariably, there is also the student who can turn a lesson into a numbers game.

When these seemingly undesirable and meaningless behaviors present themselves, they are also a direct indicator of whether your lesson reached the intended target– "the learner." A good question for the educator to ask is, "Why is all of this happening in my classroom?" A better question is, "Have I engaged or involved the learner?" More important than covering the context is ensuring that the context reached the learner.

Every teacher has had the experience where information was taught and tested but later when asked, the students could not recall the information, much less apply it to their daily lives. Learning had not taken place. Information had been disseminated but learning was bypassed. When this happens, either the teacher omitted the building blocks for retention (connecting it to something students commonly know) or the participation of the student was nil (characteristic of one way lectures).

Teaching is a process of repeating and repeating until learning takes place. The error is in the misinterpretation that teachers are the only ones repeating and/or the repeating is done in the same manner. Students are major resources and can be great contributors to the learning process. Contrary to popular belief, they desire to be an integral part of their education. When they are precluded from the process, unwanted behaviors result and learning becomes a chore rather than a joy. Review the theory of intelligence on the following pages to find useful ways to identify your resources and include your students in the educational process.

Multiple Intelligences – Simply Put

In 1983 a Harvard Professor, Howard Gardner, introduced a theory of Multiple Intelligence (MI). Citing the narrow scope by which we standardly measure intelligence, he introduced seven basic ways of knowing/learning. Commonly referred to as "smarts," Howard noted Verbal Linguistic, Spatial Intelligence, Logical Mathematical, Musical Rhythmic, Bodily Kinesthetic, Intrapersonal and Interpersonal Intelligences. Later two more intelligences were introduced: the Naturalistic and Existential Intelligences. Per Gardener, everyone has a unique mix of all intelligence; however, some "smarts" may be more predominant than others.

Part of knowing your audience is the ability to identify their "smarts". Students have a built-in way of knowing (learning) that must be identified to extract their best. The focus must transition from teaching to learning. The goal of good teaching is that it increases learning among students. The lesson plan is a great guide and a necessary one. However, most lesson plans are one-way monologues. They are full of what teachers desire to teach. The student's input is rarely addressed because it is incalculable during the lesson plan phase unless the teacher knows the audience.

Basic student behaviors identify their "smarts" or intelligence. Students that talk repeatedly are not typically doing so maliciously. They are demonstrating *Verbal Linguistic Intelligence* (word smart) and sharing their ability to contribute to the learning process. Their talking directs others to the area of their ability. The teacher's goal must be to redirect the negative behavior to a positive benefit. Trying to change the word smart student, even silence them, in a 45-50 minute period can prove to be impossible. It could also be disheartening or discouraging to the student whose intelligence has been squelched in the presence of his/her peers. The better option is to involve them. Allow them to be responsible for their education. Allow the student to become your resource.

Great teachers not only see their resource, they determine how to utilize them. Assigning the talkers to, in their own words, summarize the lesson for their classmates fulfills two goals. The *talker* is engaged in conversation (their goal), but the conversation is pertinent to the lesson and your goal, teaching. Allow every talker to give a summary, requiring them to add something different than what was previously stated. To keep interest high, add the incentive of extra points for good summaries.

Teenagers listen to their peers. They often deem them more reliable resources than their parents and teachers. Because students often speak a language unique to themselves summaries given by their peers may better explain the lesson for the students and help them to remember.

The next resource we identified was the *mover*. These students are constantly walking around the classroom; whether to the trashcan, to the computers or to the teacher's desk. They find it especially difficult to stay seated even when requested. This is **Bodily Kinesthetic Intelligence** (body smart) identifying itself in the classroom. They have an abundance of kinesthetic energy and need a way to use it. Their goal is not to be disruptive but simply to use energy. Whether the cause is due to the cereal they ate, the coffee they drank or the medication they take, the energy exists in your classroom. They are your audience so put that energy to work. Assign them to create a dance, cheer, step or exercise to help the students remember the key points in your lesson. Reward good actions with a few extra credit points and incentives.

They reach their goal to move and the teacher's goal is met because their movement is associated with the learning process. The cheers, dances, and steps created by children can absolutely amaze you. These talents are untapped until someone uses them and incorporates them in the learning process. Then the opportunity also exists for the teacher to learn from their students.

The *hummer* is often humming a song, drumming or tapping on the desk, maybe even tapping their foot. Rather than allow the extra sounds in the room to be a distraction, use them to add music to your classroom. This is **Musical Rhythmic Intelligence** (music smart) identifying itself. The hummer could simply be assigned to take your lesson and make a jingle, song or develop an acronym to help students remember. Others might add a beat to supplement the song or jingle. This allows the students to put their musical intelligence to work and gives them an opportunity to share in a way that is not a distraction to the class.

Music has a significant role in the lives of people in general. It has the ability to set a mood or fix an emotional state. Music is such an integral part of this generation that incorporating it in the classroom is almost a surefire way to gain a student's attention. If utilized properly, the creative abilities will stun the teacher and students.

A jingle was developed for preschoolers to learn the sounds of vowels in their long and short form. The jingle and the drum beat, tapped out on the desk are still with me some 20+ years later. I cannot express the joy on their little faces and the movement of their bodies when the beats got started. They were happy and learning. What a tremendous combination! They also turned out to be great readers because they knew and understood the rules for vowel sounds.

Memory also recalls a high school class memorizing the order of United States presidents through a jingle set to the music of the Beverly Hillbillies. By learning from each other, they were successful on the test. Singing was part of their study pattern.

The *quiet, attentive, copious note taker* who rarely socializes is **Intrapersonal Intelligence** in action. These students are in tune with their own feelings, thoughts and goals. Customarily, the *Intrapersonal Intelligence* (self smart) student is the model student for traditional education. Behaviorally, they are the best. Unwittingly, most teachers develop lesson plans that meet the instructional needs of the Intrapersonal (self smart) student. Note that 83% of teachers wanted these types of students in their classrooms, according to the Public Agenda Poll.

The recommendation is to use their consistency as a resource. Assign this student to create puzzles, study worksheets, and note cards for the class based on the lessons. An even more creative outlet might be to write a skit that can be enacted by the kinesthetic group. Compare the skits, puzzles, worksheets and note cards created by the verbal learner and give extra points for the most creative and accurate ones.

When they are drawing, the *doodlers* rarely appear to pay attention when, in fact, they are demonstrating ***Spatial Intelligence*** (picture smart). Students with Spatial Intelligence can illustrate your lesson. They could be assigned to develop a funny cartoon or sketch to share with the class. The cartoon should include key study points or key statements for upcoming lessons, tests or quizzes.

The key is that every student has the opportunity to become a participant in the learning process, not simply a bystander or receiver. An additional bonus exists because each opportunity to create and present helps students to develop their presentation skills. Language skills are developed and retention is multiplied at the same time the lesson plan is being reviewed.

The ***Logical/ Mathematical Intelligence*** (logic smart) student can easily re-teach or build calculations for the math classes. In other classes they might be charged to keep the statistics or grading logs. They will be the ones to determine that three of your major terms begin with the letter "A" and seven begin with the letter "C". In any way that mathematical information can enhance your lesson, the logical mathematical student is your in-class resource.

The *socialite* or student who appears to easily talk, cooperate and work with others typically has ***Interpersonal Intelligence*** (people smart) at work. Group work excites this learner. The opportunity to share knowledge and interact with others is a key to their success. Team work is important to them and they know how to motivate others to perform their duties. They often present well and have great oratory skills.

As a teacher you may choose to grade the summary, grade the jingle, grade the puzzle, and/or grade the illustrations. You might also grant extra points for presentations to keep your students involved in the lesson. The key is that you see your lesson plan through their eyes. When you do, one can easily answer the question, did learning take place in my classroom?" The answer is probably a resounding, YES!

What are the benefits of an interactive classroom?

❖ Peer- to-peer instruction
❖ Increased student participation
❖ Increased retention of information
❖ An opportunity to learn innovative ideas from your students
❖ An opportunity to learn more about your audience; thereby gaining the information necessary to properly instruct them
❖ An unplanned appreciation for student's talents and abilities
❖ Redeeming the time commonly dedicated to behavior correction and modification (Don't fight them, use them. Give them an engaging assignment.)

Resources are only good when one recognizes that they are available and chooses to utilize them. In addition to the book, board, chairs and desks, every teacher has a classroom filled with living, breathing resources. Each student is a resource. Consider the knowledge and experience in your room. What they bring to the learning environment can assist the educator in fulfilling the charge to education. With them is a wealth of knowledge and experience that can make each lesson an exciting adventure.

What You Bring to the Learning Experience

Some years ago I was assigned to teach both the 7th and 8th grade math classes. The 8th grade class was algebra one. I was employed in a Christian school that separated the boys from the girls until high school. My 7th grade math students were failing miserably. There were approximately twenty males and, with the exception of maybe three, they were failing. I did not like these results nor did I want to be responsible for failing to equip this group of young men.

I knew the subject matter. I prepared my lesson plans, kept up with grading, gave adequate quizzes to give opportunities for grade improvement. I answered every question they had, and repeated the lessons as they had need. I even created a math project equivalent to one test grade to boost their interest and grades; yet there was very little interest.

One day I looked at my class and realized that these were sons, brothers and uncles, not just students. I stretched my imaginations to fathers and husbands who could not balance a checkbook and professionals who would not manage their finances. My imaginations stretched to dishonest financiers stealing all their earnings. I saw individuals who would be cheated out of the correct change at the store and entrepreneurs whose dreams were stolen because they did not count the cost. I remembered the Leaning Tower of Pisa whose appearance is definitely a mathematic miscalculation. As I considered what I perceived in my own mind, I felt responsible to change and change quickly.

I went to the Director of Education, who happened to be the person responsible for the Teacher Training Class required by all educators in our school. I had learned so much from her class that I was sure she would have an answer. She listened to my situation very intently. I ended my explanation with, "How can I get my students to love math, understand its necessity, and make it applicable to their lives?" Instead of giving me answers, she smiled and simply asked me questions. "Do you love math? Do you find it necessary and applicable to your life?"

She inferred that my students would feed off the energy that I brought to the classroom. If I wanted them to enjoy math, I needed to enjoy math. If I wanted them to apply it to life, I had to teach them to apply it to life. If I wanted them to understand that math was necessary, I needed to show them how necessary it was. In short, it was my job to raise their level of interest in the subject matter. Their learning was my responsibility.

From that very moment, my math and algebra classes changed. I only used the book as a reference to what we were to teach. I began to use their personal interests and life circumstances, which completely changed how I taught the material. Because of the different approach, more material was covered than had been previously. I continued to sharpen my skills by watching math videos on the educational channel. I was determined to make myself a better teacher to help them become better students.

Knowing the subject matter is a small part of teaching. *You must know your audience* and what is pertinent to them. There are some basic things most children have in common. Start there and build. *Recall* is best when it is connected to something students already know. Every lesson should build on an existing foundation. Knowing your audience helps you locate that foundation and successfully build upon it.

I requested permission to separate the teaching materials in two categories. I labeled one *Need to Know* and the other *Nice to Know*. After briefly reviewing the 9th grade Algebra II book to confirm that necessary material was not improperly categorized as *Nice to Know*, I began to work. We dove heavily into the *Need to Know* using as many possible life situations to help them build their understanding of when to use mathematical methods and why. We inserted *Nice to Know* material when time and circumstance permitted. Lessons in both classes became relevant to the learner.

For example, each student had to choose a career goal. Then they had to research the math required to achieve the profession and how it was used in that profession. *I learned this from the educational channel*. It was amazing that every job chosen required mathematics of some kind. Only then did math become pertinent to daily life.

Several students wanted to be professional ball players and were excited about the money attached to signed contracts. For the sake of conjecture, I asked how much money they thought an owner made per game. We calculated the income from tickets sold in the nearest arena all the way to the nose bleed seats. We included contracts from vendors, skybox seats purchased by corporations and so on. The number was staggering. Then they understood how an athlete could make a few million. It was a great time in math.

My students learned that math applied to everything. By the end of the school year, they were changed and so was I. To assuage my past failure to see their needs over the lesson plan, I offered six Saturdays from 9:00AM-

12:00PM at the local library. During these sessions, we reviewed previous math lessons to prepare them for the final and the last six-week grading period.

I recognized that it was not the student's fault that I lacked experience and was not able to see their needs above the need to cover the lesson plan. Nor was it the students fault that my lesson plans were not relevant to their lives; thereby, giving them no desire to learn the material. I could not allow students to fail because I failed to be a good teacher. So I offered my time, my new found perception of life applicable math and began to instruct at the library on Saturdays.

The parents and students were excited that there was an opportunity for success. Even though there were students whose parents' schedules conflicted with the six-week library sessions, according to my recollection, only three students ended the year without a passing math grade. Regardless of the grades, we were all changed.

Learning became relevant, fun and interesting. My students became active participants rather than an audience for preplanned lessons. I became a better person and a better teacher once I learned that *education was for the children.*

The Table in the Back of the Room
& the Teacher's Aide

Many years ago when I was in elementary school, we had a large table in the back of the room for SRA reading books. When we completed our assignments we could leave our seats and go to the table to select color coded reading materials. Each color represented a different level of achievement in student paced learning. At the end of the school year, the level each of us had achieved was announced. The teacher's aide would check our reading level periodically and was available to assist with any questions we might have about proceeding through the levels.

While in the 4th grade, I remember hearing it announced that I read on a 7th grade level based on the SRA reading books. One student in my class read at the 8th grade level. We were the top two students. I was surprised to learn that, without my knowledge, I was achieving something. I was just reading because I enjoyed it. Many of the students in my class never made it to the back table because they needed more time to complete their assigned work or found no interest in reading additional stories.

This was *at will* learning that created no schisms or elite class perception among us. At no time did I feel smarter or less smart than my fellow classmates. I was not singled out as bright and gifted or otherwise. It was a single line of achievement announced on the last day of school during the class party. We would exit the building for the summer, not looking to judge the capabilities of others but preparing to enjoy summer. There was no class system in education, it was just our class.

Today, the gifted, college bound, and honor students are separated from the rest of their peers. Our educational system has created a caste system within itself capable of crushing the forward progress of many and overlooking the value of self-paced learning while remaining within the group. A single test or a few percent grade averages either open or close the door to achievement for an entire school year or even a future.

It was the teacher's aide who manned the table in the back who occasionally answered questions and helped us move forward. Our regular teacher never came to the back. She concentrated on the other students. Should our current system invest in the teacher's aide at the table in the back, many classroom dynamics would change for the better.

I bring to your remembrance the table of Algebra II students who enlisted my help to understand the material. The substitute teacher was running from table to table and did not have enough time to reach every table. The students left the class without understanding the material needed to do their homework. The teacher had no time to help them, and they had admitted that their parents and siblings did not understand the material. They felt doomed to fail. Yet, they had the tenacity to request the help of a complete stranger – me.

Teach Because I Came!

The presence of a knowledgeable teacher's aide could have completely changed their Algebra II experience. There were too many students for one teacher to manage, particularly when gaps in their knowledge made the lesson even more challenging. This became evident when there were so many questions after the introduction of the assignment.

This educational plan proposes that the *table in the back* of the classroom should be manned daily by the teacher's aide and used during independent practice for students who require additional help. After the teacher completes the lesson plan and students begin the independent practice, students who require more attention and help should immediately come to this table. In the current classroom environment the struggling students compete with 30 other students by raising their hand to signal that they need more help. The time wasted waiting to be the next student who gets attention cannot be regained. The *table in the back* allows those students who need extra help to immediately go there to receive help from the teacher's aide.

Immediate help after instruction provides many benefits for the student and ultimately for the entire class. It can prevent gaps in understanding and prevent long-term storage of misinformation. It can also serve as a real-time, didactic gauge to measure the successfulness of the lesson plan. This type of support can also help the class move as a unit rather than disjointedly. A knowledgeable teacher's aide can assist the students until they are capable of successful and confident independent practice. For the price of only one competent teacher's aide, students are provided the advantage of having an in-class tutor.

For budget strapped communities, students who excel in math could also assist to fulfill the need for extra instruction or practice. Local colleges with students majoring in the subject matter could assign a period of time (quarter, semester or year) as a teacher's aide for graduation requirements. Parent volunteers can also be of great help in this area. The prevailing idea is that help is needed and there are multiple ways to provide that assistance for our students.

Lessons where 20-30% of the class need help from the *table in the back* is a lesson that must be re-taught. The teacher's aide will be able to gauge the level of assistance given from the table, and the teacher should be able to determine the need from the questions received from the students. Together they should determine if the lesson must be re-taught and/or reviewed before new material is presented.

The four-fold NAPP program for Academics includes the daily support of a *teacher's aide* and *the table in the back* for every classroom. Both are viewed as a necessity to the educational process rather than a luxury. With the proper perspective, such aide could become an in-time tutoring tool for students who need more assistance.

Summer School

The NAPP program is designed for academic excellence for all students. With high expectations for success, summer school is an inherent part of the program required for all students functioning at a C grade level or below. Each department (math, science, history, English, etc.) is required to establish a team that will properly train students in the designated subject areas for six weeks in the summer.

Designated Subject Groups (DSG's)

Designated Subject Groups (DSG's) are a collection of teachers from like subject areas who are responsible for the overall instruction of students in that subject as well as the development of teachers who will teach the assigned subjects. DSG's are established to ultimately hold teachers responsible for the success of their students through the creation of peer review and pooling of academic resources as a basis for student achievement.

The purpose of the Designated Subject Groups is threefold:

(1) To develop continuity of information progression through grade levels,

(2) To establish excellent teacher training, including optimum lesson presentation techniques

(3) To development class management skills

Using a Mathematics Designated Subject Group (MDSG), as an example, the MDSG would first combine all math teachers from basic math to trigonometry and calculus into one group. Their purpose will be to first evaluate the tools they are using (books, lessons, etc.) to insure that there is no gap in information or instruction from one grade level to the next. Then collectively they must determine which skills are paramount and must be mastered to be successful in the next grade level of mathematics. They will distinguish the *need to know* from the *nice to know* to ensure student success.

With the goal of adequately preparing all teachers within the designated subject groups to successfully instruct mathematics, peer review of teacher instruction will be conducted. Each teacher must teach a minimum of three times to his/her peers within the designated subject groups before the school year begins and periodic peer reviews would continue throughout the school year. With student participation as the hallmark for instructions, teachers will exchange ideas, recommend teaching tools, share visual aids and prepare their specific groups to teach.

The DSG's will also avail themselves during the six week summer school program to help prepare students to succeed. Students with grades C or lower will be automatically enrolled in summer school and evaluated to determine their weaknesses during the summer program. A cadre of concepts from basic mathematical concepts through to algebraic equations (or applicable math level) will be reviewed. The purpose will be to fill the gaps in knowledge and re-teach failed concepts.

In the mathematics summer program, it is conceivable that the student could have up to six different teachers during the six weeks program. Each teacher would concentrate on a week of mastering the basic concepts of their area. For example the first week would include basic mathematics to include addition/division of fractions, pre-algebraic operations; the second week geometric equations; the third week mastery of those two concepts; weeks four, five and six would be concentration of algebra I & II, trigonometry, pre-calculus and calculus.

The same process would exist for English Designated Subject Groups. Week one could conceivably include basic sentence structure and parts of speech; Week two, paragraph development; Week three, development of essays and short stories; Weeks four through six, report writing, etc.

Different teachers would teach each week drilling their sections to ensure that the *need to know* information has been mastered. All students should be confident in their abilities and prepared to function at grade level by the end of summer school. With the DSG's being responsible for student success, the anticipated outcome is improved student success, improved quality of instruction and educational accountability.

Designated subject groups would be offered each summer in the main areas of study such as English, Mathematics, Science and History. Reading and comprehension classes may also be developed for various grade levels as needed. Ultimately the goal is to transition to each new grade level fully prepared for the academic requirements.

Classroom Monitors

One cannot overexpress the tremendous value of non-biased classroom monitors. Many times principals and department heads are too busy to monitor classrooms and evaluate lesson plans. This is a critical component necessary to increase accountability, share valuable information, and improve the teaching skills of school employees. NAPP would require a minimum of 3-4 evaluations per year for each teacher/instructor.

Though strategically planned by the monitors, the visits should not be scheduled with the teacher or local administration. Teachers should be provided immediate feedback on their lessons and classroom management with commendations as well as recommendations for improvements as determined. Principals will receive a copy of the evaluations and assist in making recommendations for improvement. After each evaluation the monitor should follow up to ensure that the teacher has adhered to the recommendations.

Nutrition Academics Physical Psychosocial (NAPP) Program

Physical Education

Studies have long supported the value of physical education in children and adults. Regular physical activity has a beneficial effect on the body as a whole and reduces the likelihood of diseases such as obesity, cancer, heart disease and diabetes.[44] Studies have also linked physical activity with brain growth as well as with the secretion of dopamine (the neurotransmitter that governs pleasure).

The section on *Nutrition* revealed startling statistics on childhood obesity. To reiterate, the *2012 Statistical Fact Sheet* for the American Heart Association and American Stroke Association indicates that one in three children between ages 2-19 is either overweight or obese. One in six children is obese in America.[45] It is estimated that the cost of obesity will be 254 billion dollars between 2020 through 2050 (includes medical cost and loss of

---

[44] Berg, Kris. *Justifying Physical Education Based on Neuroscience Evidence*, JOPERD. March 2010.
<http://www.aahperd.org/publications/journals/joperd/justifying-physical-education-based-on-neuroscience-evidence.cfm> (accessed May 2012).
[45] American Heart Association/ American Stroke Association, "Statistical Fact Sheet 2012 Update – Overweight and Obesity,"
<http://www.heart.org/idc/groups/heart-public/@wcm/@sop/@smd/documents/downloadable/ucm_319588.pdf>
(accessed May 2012).

productivity). With statistics like these, physical education can no longer be optional - it is a necessity.

Many schools only provide physical education programs up to the 9th grade, leaving three years of inactivity before a student leaves high school. The booming technological information age, wherein the entire body is sedentary with the exception of the hands, is a major contributor to the inactivity of our children. Television, computers, video games, and cellular technology are all managed from sedentary postures. They all increase our level of inactivity.

The NAPP Program proposes physical education classes, minimally three times a week throughout the school years, spanning elementary to high school graduation. As with nutrition, physical education should be a federally funded program because obesity is a national epidemic with great possibility of remedy within the school system. The relief to our health care system and disease index should be sufficient rationale to fund the program perpetually.

President Kennedy's Physical Fitness program and other similar programs were enacted because Americans were becoming bigger than ever before in history. NAPP recommends the inclusion of this type of physical fitness program.

I personally remember President Kennedy's physical fitness program being followed at our middle school. We had to run a mile under 10 minutes, do push-ups, sit ups, and learn to play all sports, including gymnastics. We had to participate in gym three times a week and on those three days we managed to exercise, shower and be dressed for our next class within 60 minutes.

The benefits of physical exercise are numerous. To name a few, physical exercise increases muscle tone and physical strength, promotes good oxygen circulation to the brain to increase learning, increases personal confidence, helps prevent disease, and inspires team cooperation in organized sports. NAPP regards physical exercise as critically as it does academic excellence.

Nutrition Academics Physical Psychosocial (NAPP) Program

Psychosocial Services and Referrals

In light of the statistical review of Generation Z it became abundantly clear that the scope of educational services must expand to include referral services such as Psychologists, Licensed Professional Counselors, and Child Protective Services. Schools typically provide academic counselors who help students chart their educational paths for the future; however, studies have shown that almost 50% of students have needs that are outliers or considered outside of the scope of the current educational system. By law, the educational arena has the student for eight hours per day and can easily add supplemental services to meet the needs of our students.

Students who would benefit from group therapy, cognitive behavioral therapy, counseling psychologists, and/or clinical psychologists would be served through this integral component of NAPP. NAPP proposes that Licensed Professional Counselors have offices on the school campuses. A major responsibility of the counselors would be to organize group counseling for students and possibly family counseling in the evenings for the families of Generation Z.

The Psychosocial components of NAPP will operate both by referral (from teacher, approved by principal) and student-sought assistance. Had such life saving counseling components been a part of the structure of Columbine High School before the tragedy of April 20, 1999 (15 died and 24 injured) or Newtown, Connecticut (26 people killed) outcomes may have been different. The shooting at Virginia Tech on April 16, 2007 (32 killed and 17 wounded) and the December 2012 massacre with James Holmes at the movie theater in Colorado (12 killed and 58 wounded) might have been thwarted had the gunmen received the counseling services necessary during their middle-school and/or high-school years.

NAPP regards the Licensed Professional Counselor (LPC) as a gateway to healing some of the hurts and challenges of Generation Z. Students will be openly informed of the services provided and given the freedom to seek the services they need without implications or repercussion, but with a certainty that their needs will be met. LPC's will engage other community services for each child as needed. Such services would include, but not be limited to, child protective services, rape crisis centers, and benefits from social services.

Successful Alternative Therapies

Alternative therapies such as EEG Biofeedback, otherwise known as neurofeedback, also provide safe and effective treatments for Attention Deficit Disorder (ADD and ADHD), depression, schizophrenia, bipolarism, learning difficulties, lack of focus, lack of concentration and much more. Neurofeedback uses the brain's ability to self-regulate and make necessary adjustments for healthy behavior. This manuscript proposes using such non-drug, non-invasive therapies to help students gain optimal brain functioning and emotional control.

Neurofeedback is typically administered in 20 session intervals lasting thirty minutes each. Baseline scores are determined at the beginning of the sessions, re-charted midway and at the end to determine overall progress. Analysis of the brain's wave patterns of beta, alpha, theta and delta helps to determine how the brain responds to stimuli. Scores will reveal the areas of the brain which are hyper-functioning or hypo-functioning. The sessions are designed to create a balanced brain which functions at optimum levels.

At the end of the twenty sessions the client is re-evaluated to determine if more sessions are required. By far, it is the most promising and effective method to enhance brain functioning without pharmaceutical drugs and their egregious side effects. This method also gives the student a sense of accomplishment through learning to self-regulate without the need for long-term drug therapy.

Instruments such as the Roshi® and pRoshi® are a tremendous asset in both therapeutic and personal home-based therapies that could greatly benefit our educational system. The brain receives instructions from the machine, via flashing lights coded to cause the brain to create pathways to self regulation and enhance abilities.

The Roshi® is a **central nervous system training** device developed to enhance the brains functionality. Created as a NeuroDynamic Activator® for both clinical (ROSHI) and personal (pROSHI) use, its purpose is to cause the brain to evaluate and repair, as needed, its processing pathways. With the goal of the brain functioning at optimum levels and peak performance, the ROSHI increases the brain's ability to function according to its original intent. Patterned after the deepest level of meditation practiced by Monks, the ROSHI also works to promote oneness in mind, body and spirit by signaling the brain into a meditative state. The ROSHI is an excellent complement to traditional Neurofeedback, promoting effective and long term benefits. It is also the optimal device for personal cognitive enhancement.

Parental Involvement
(Mandatory 20 hours per year)

Understanding that the education of our children must become a cooperative effort, the NAPP program requires that each parent, caretaker or legal guardian volunteer twenty hours each year within the school system. The school should not release the final report card until the service is fulfilled. Barring extenuating circumstances (death, chronic illness, etc.) all hours must be filled.

The education of our children can no longer be viewed as a job for the school system only but must be viewed as one that requires parental involvement. Parents will be required to spend eight of the twenty hours observing or serving in their child's classroom. The other twelve hours can be assigned at the discretion of the school administration.

With proper management, each class could have an additional daily classroom monitor with the role being fulfilled by a parent volunteer. Parents could work in areas ranging from the library, the classroom, the school office, to security and custodial services. Schools should prepare for an onslaught of volunteers and assign them to various areas as needed.

In preparation for volunteerism, each school system must develop and conduct periodic orientation classes designed to teach parents how to properly volunteer at their school. This training should include the specific rules and regulations to be followed for classroom observation. It should also provide the gateway by which schools can protect themselves through background checks.

Parents must submit to background checks before serving on the school campus. After a cleared background check, parents may fulfill their volunteer hours. Because the final report card will not be released unless the 20 hours of volunteerism are completed, those parents who fail the background check must seek assistance within their family structure to fulfill the required hours.

For those families whose structure needs more help than the immediate or extended family can provide, attendance at family group counseling may be a way to fulfill their volunteer hours. The referral from teachers, principals or student-sought counseling may stipulate that some or all parental hours be filled via counseling. Licensed counselors would prescribe the number of hours required to ensure student/family success.

The Psychosocial arm of the NAPP program allows the licensed counselors to utilize community services to strengthen the student and their families. In an effort to utilize resources and unify community services, food and clothing pantries may be contacted to assist families. Referrals may also include local churches or faith organizations to help families develop a sound moral compass and who may also provide parenting classes. Community Action referrals may range from budgeting classes to helping parents manage their income, to drug and alcohol rehabilitation centers assigned to help overcome addictions. With its goal being singular - to meet the needs of the students - this branch can extend beyond the standard educational border.

Realm of Possibilities:

In the cul-de-sac of my neighborhood spanning a 1-2 block perimeter were five families with students who attended the same high school. For the first time in our family, one of our children went to a school in the area where we lived. One morning as the garage door opened and we waved at parents who were going to the same destination, the questions of possibilities flooded my mind.

What if we shared ride responsibilities? What if we took turns in the classrooms on our day off or used one week of vacation to show parental presence in the school system? What if another parent were able to make the same positive deposit in the life of my child that the Caring Teacher and I chose to make in the life of Trina Z and others? What if we all came to the conclusion that we do not know what current-day high school looks like, but we can listen to our children and learn? What if parental presence and input were one of the critical missing components in public schools? If we knew this for certain, then certainly every caring parent would do his/her share.

Confirmation of Purpose

On an ordinary day off, when I began to chronicle the experience of high school at age 51, I paused to examine the depth of the task at hand. Questioning my own abilities, I plunged ahead with full steam, recognizing that I was simply a conduit, a vessel for a larger purpose than myself or my family. Humbled to have been chosen for the experience, I wrote with unbridled certainty that these experiences would help someone.

At the end of the day, not having accomplished as much as I would have liked, I received an encouraging motivation to continue. Football season was over for my high school senior; therefore, he was home early with much to talk about.

"Mom, was today your day off?" he asked.

"Yes, it is," I responded.

"The students are asking about you," he informed me.

"What students?" I questioned really puzzled.

"All of them, mostly the ones that were in my Algebra II class before I changed."

"What are they saying?"

"They say, 'Hey Jay, Where is your Mom? We miss her. *They only teach when she comes.* I wish she would come back.' "

I sat down on the staircase, my place of epiphany. This time tears dropped from my eyes. Unbeknown to him, he confirmed the title of the book, *"Teach Because I Came."*

"Now what, Mom?" he asked, recognizing my mood change.

"Son, did I stop going too soon? Was I selfish in simply staying until your situation was stabilized? Was my only concern you and not the other 150 students I encountered daily? That was pretty selfish."

"I don't know, Mom. You can come back if you want to. But I am okay. Maybe what you have to do is bigger than my school. You said it was bigger than me.

Do the bigger thing, Mom. I think that means it will help everybody. Maybe it just started with me, because I'm special, huh?" he playfully asked.

"Yes, you are. No doubt about it. You are one of a kind," I replied, smiling.

We hugged and he walked away. Compelled to change the mood of my disappointment, he yelled from a distance, "By the way, the girls at school think I'm sexy."

Smirking, I replied, "By the way, I'm your Mom and that thought will never enter my mind about you."

Laughing, he responded with, "Mom, the girls say that even my baby pictures *(taken to school for a project)* are sexy. I have been sexy for a long time. I know you noticed."

"You mean the ones slobbering from teething, the ones wearing diapers, or the ones wearing bow ties for preschool pictures? Those are sexy?"

"Yes, those are the ones!" Jay proudly reported. Laughter broke out on both sides.

"Well, alright. If that is sexy, you are safe, and so am I. Love you Son."

"Love you too, Mom." After a moment of thinking, he continued with, "Mom, when you do the *bigger* thing, will I be rich?"

"No, Son. You will be rich when *you* do the bigger thing. So get started."

"I am still sexy."

I smiled in amazement at his ability to discern a situation and properly respond. I developed a new found respect for this invaluable ability. Such a quality is capable of bringing nations to peaceful solutions; however, in our current educational system, it might not show up as class valedictorian. I prayed that somehow he would always use it for the good of all.

My interpretation of this title which quietly entered the thoughts of my mind the first day of my high school visit was not to teach *because I came, but because the students came.* However in one poignant moment, both student and parent came to learn and left unfulfilled. As a result, I have determined that the parental responsibility to education is greater than our tax dollars. We have to do better than send our children to school. We have to *show up* for the betterment of all students.

The Call to Unity

The solution to our nation's educational woes is multifaceted. The educational system cannot do it alone. The home/family environment cannot do it alone. Social and religious services cannot accomplish the task alone. There must be a unification of efforts and a blending of goals for the welfare of our children.

Parental endeavors, with the best of intentions, may not be successful without the help of a good school. Educational goals and objectives are unattainable without the help of good responsible parents and/or guardians. Community plans and developments (services, churches, businesses, and activities) are not sustainable without educated, responsible citizens. This illustration of interconnectedness continues to the state and national level. When either area of responsibility fails to do its part, other areas are affected and suffer tremendously.

Each entity in a child's life is responsible to give its best and to do its best on behalf of our children. A unification of school, home and community is necessary to give our students the best and to extract from them their best efforts.

First and foremost in the *unification* is the commitment to "put away the pointing of the finger." Blaming the school, the teachers, the parents or the community will not yield progress. History has proven this repeatedly. The blame game keeps entities that should work together at odds with one another. The home, school and community must make a concerted effort to respect each other's deposit in the life of a student. The return on the investment from all entities will outgrow the sum of its parts if properly respected and nurtured.

As it relates to the education of our children, both home and school could take a page from the old *"one room school house"* practiced in earlier societies. Teachers taught their students with no hope of help from the parents because most were unlearned and uneducated manual laborers. Parents raised their children to be responsible, honest, trustworthy, hardworking and respectful. Parents taught their children everything they knew, not necessarily by book and pen, but by moral conduct, discipline, dedication, skill and trade. Both the home and the school did their part to contribute to the overall development of the individual.

The role of the church in earlier societies was significant in developing moral character and integrity. Much of our constitution was built on Biblical principles. Both the church and school maximized what they had for the benefit of the nation. Individuals of great intellectual and moral character were the ultimate fruit of each entity giving its best. The collective productivity of these individuals built this nation.

Primed to produce the best nation, none blamed the others but respected the expertise, knowledge and experience that each could bring to the development of a well rounded individual. The message is simply to do your assignment, whether teacher or parent, or civic leader, without expectation of another.

In the early day, the teacher knew that it was the student who would return home to teach the family the *book learning* they received in the classroom. Most families could only afford to allow one child to go to school to be educated. The others were needed for survival of the family either in the field or elsewhere on the farm. Though our society has progressed to technological marvels, this core aspect of education must remain the same. Each entity brings the best that it can offer to a child's overall educational experience.

A real time example of why this is necessary occurred while I sat in an Algebra II class at 7:30 AM. The students were completely confused about how to complete their in-class assignment. The substitute solved an algebraic equation on the boards. The solution to one problem spanned two large white boards in the classroom. When I say there was writing over every inch of those boards, believe me. The class was asked to repeat the same process for each problem on the handout they were given.

A student leaned to me, the visitor in the back of classroom and whispered, "Do you understand this?" I smiled and honestly responded, "No."

"Have you ever taken Algebra?" they asked.

"Yes, I have and I did very well. But I am sorry, I do not understand this." Instantly I knew it was not because I could not understand, but the presentation of two large white boards as the solution to one problem caused my brain to shut down as it did the students in the classroom.

Before I could complete my next statement, which was going to be "Ask the teacher," another student chimed in and stated, "My parents do not understand either. I ask them to help me and they look at the book for a long time, but they do not understand. My older brother took Algebra II and did well but he said they are not teaching it the same. I have no help outside the classroom." Two other students chimed in and said, "Me neither."

This is an example of why blaming the parents for a student's failure is convenient, but short sighted. In this case, parents were expected to be able to teach their child in areas in which they are neither trained nor certified. It is painful for me to have my child ask for help academically, and even with your degrees and training, find myself unable to provide it. Magnify the inability to provide that necessary help with the thought that your lack of knowledge may contribute to your child's possible failing grade. Further magnify the outcome to the possibility of affecting a student's acceptance into college. Consider that the *new math* has rendered many parents helpless in the homework arena. Then consider what can be done to help.

One private school immediately saw this kind of dilemma and offered a one-hour class twice a week. The goal was to provide the students with additional help in the evenings. The pre-calculus teacher was astute enough to know that, without help, most parents could not offer the support necessary. He not only availed himself to his students but also to their parents. To those parents who were able to take advantage of this offer, it afforded their child a refresher to the earlier lesson and served as an introduction for the parents. For the parents who attended with their child, it was a successful venture.

Irony and the School Board Meeting

We talk much about the value of education and how important it is for Americans to successfully compete on the world's platform. We link quality education to life-changing discoveries, inventions and solutions to the unexplained. There is constant conversation about the need for greater investment and well trained educators for America's educational system; yet, our actions often undermine the very foundation of such statements.

While sitting in a clandestinely planned school board meeting, I was puzzled by the words and actions of those who governed the school district. My attendance was in response to a plea from the high school counselors, who asked if I would come and speak on their behalf. My recent tenure in high school gave me an up-close view of their job responsibilities and the great value that school counselors single-handedly add to the educational process. Reluctantly, I agreed. *Disbelief* is the only word that accurately summarizes my view of the school board meeting experience. I simply refused to believe that what I witnessed that Tuesday evening was the best we could offer our students.

The week prior to my attendance, the school board agenda contained a proposal for laying off all high school counselors. When the students in the district learned of it, they showed up to protest in full force. Because, they spoke so eloquently and with such passion, the school board promised they would not lay off the counselors.

They thanked the students for their commitment to their own education and their willingness to support the school counselors. The very next week the school board held an unpublicized, emergency meeting proposing layoffs of the librarians, coaching staff, and *high school counselors* again. Emergency meetings were called within 24 hours.

Notification to the schools within the district was within a short time frame to avoid the backlash of the previous meeting. Students receive an announcement over the school's intercom that the high school counselor's situation, which they thought was resolved, was up for discussion again. In like fashion, they showed up in numbers again. Therefore, the tone of this meeting was quite different from the last.

Students who were in attendance were angry and felt betrayed by the school board. While students supported their high school counselors, coaches and librarians, they also questioned the integrity of the board. More than a few students bluntly called the board liars, indicating that just one week prior, they promised to keep high school counselors and the next week they broke their promise. The students openly questioned the School Board's trustworthiness.

Tempers were soaring and the School Board became defensive, indicating that they felt insulted by the students. Shortly afterwards, it was my turn to speak. In fear and trembling, I approached the podium.

I started by saying, "We constantly teach our children about the importance of education and justly so.

However, I believe that our scope of education is limited to the view of students, teachers and textbooks. I believe we overlook the glue that holds the entire process together. That glue is the high school counselor. They are the gateway to the future for many students and a bridge to success for the present time."

I continued my presentation by pointing out that many details fall under the prevue of the high school counselor. To name a few:

Counselors are responsible for:

- ❖ course selection at each high school grade level to assure that graduation requirements are met.
- ❖ the processes to change and add classes. They are the first to know the overall successes and failures of students and are required to respond accordingly.
- ❖ contacting parents when students are failing or in danger of not progressing to the next level. They meet with parents and students to determine the problems and provide solutions.
- ❖ being the bridge between the students and the teachers. When a student is missing the mark or chronically absent, getting them on track is the work of the school counselor. Teachers send students to the counselors when they are having a difficult time socially or emotionally.

❖ reporting child abuse and child endangerment. Counselors are informed when a student is hungry and has no food at home, or if the lights are cut off, or if there is no running water in the home. They know when home-life conflicts with school life.

❖ Connecting students to the proper services.

Cases that require the expertise of a school counselor are relocations. Students who have been relocated from other states or school districts need the school counselor to match classes/credits to ensure that the newly relocated student is able to meet the requirements for graduation. This my family knew from first-hand experience. Considerable work is involved because course title alone did not satisfy the guidelines for credit acceptance. It was the school counselor who contacted the necessary persons to determine if the classes from another state met the requirements for the current state with regard to graduation.

Couple the aforementioned workload for counselors with the housing market crash. The number of students who relocated because they lost their homes is staggering. The weight of their entry into any new school system is in the hands of the high school counselor. Then imagine a school system with no entity in place to handle this overwhelming need. That is exactly what our school board was proposing.

High school counselors are the first line of contact and defense for students who enter the system without parents. Students who are wards of the state, who live in group homes or who are placed in foster care are assigned to counselors with the appropriate background information submitted. High school counselors often become the person who extends an arm of care and encourages students to finish high school. They work to instill a belief that students can accomplish anything if they are willing to work hard and finish.

Some students have no idea what to do with their futures. It is the counselor that causes many students to begin to consider life after high school. They are great planters of visions for college and life careers. They research the college requirements and meet with students, collectively and individually, to impart vital information. They are the writers of most letters of recommendations for college entry. Counselors often help students find colleges that offer the major of choice. They extend their efforts to include applications for scholarships and financial aid.

When I spoke of my personal experience with a high school counselor, before the school board and everyone in the audience, my tears began to flow. My family had moved to a new state. I felt rather alone and the social adjustment was more than I knew how to handle. It was my high school counselor who informed me that I was college material. He was the first to inquire of my future plans. He presented me with a list of colleges and suggested that I apply to a few of the colleges on the list.

I applied to two. He wrote the letters of recommendation to each college.

I began to weep because, for the first time, I remembered the deposit that this unassuming man, the high school counselor, made in my life. He was the first person to tell me I was smart enough to go to college. He opened the door to my future and encouraged me to walk through. At that moment, I was overwhelmed with gratitude and saw the incredible deposit that a school counselor could make in the life of a student.

I reminded them that most high school students do not inform parents of scheduled parent meetings or parent-teacher meeting. It is the high school counselor. There are several mandatory meetings that the student and parent must attend for the student to graduate. It is the high school counselor that prioritizes their time to inform the parents.

History has shown that information given to a student often stays in the backpack or finds its way to the trash. Social and technological issues are of greater concern to them at this stage of their development. Therefore, the autodialing products that most school systems purchase, and the automated online parent connects to view grades and progress, are necessary because students typically do not bring pertinent papers home to their parents.

At the board meeting, I openly confessed that it was the high school counselor that extended the offer for a parent to come to school and see what happens in the course of my student's day. I attributed the success of my high school senior to the counselor. She was the person that made sure his credits from another state counted. She was the person that informed me that he had more credits than needed to graduate; however, he was struggling in a particular class that was necessary for a university versus a state college. I was unaware that such a distinction existed. She was the person that kept me in the high school loop. I both needed and respected her contribution to the success of my son. It was unimaginable that other students might be without the same quality of assistance.

When one considers four high school counselors for a student body of 1200, the case load *(300 students per counselor)* becomes clear. To contemplate taking away the *glue* in the process was less than wise and more damaging than one might perceive especially when the primary focus is balancing the school budget. Too many lives unnamed and without faces, were not being weighed in the balance of a right decision from the School Board.

In a previous presentation, a gentleman calculated that if each person in the school district took a $200.00 cut in pay, each entity targeted for lay-offs (counselors, librarians and coaches) could keep their jobs. I was moved to ask, "How many would give up $200.00 to keep every person on staff?" The response was unanimous. In summary, I reminded the board that the solution was right there before them. A one-time, $200.00 cut in yearly salary, approximately $16.66 per month, would solve the problem. I thanked them for their time and moved toward the door. It was almost 10:00PM and the meeting was still in process.

This school board meeting was undeniable proof that students are not sleeping during the educational process, as had been proclaimed. Students do care and are willing to fight for their education and for every component in the process. It was clear, as it was 35 years ago, that the high school counselor is the primary gateway to graduation and college. The counselor's unique vantage point to encourage is without the parental pressure of what a student should become, but simply the possibility of what could be. This, in itself, is invaluable in the life of a child.

As I exited the podium, I noticed that my otherwise cool, unengaged son was standing near me. He put his arms around my shoulder, hugged me and uttered, "I am proud of you, Mom. You did a good job."

I apologized for crying before the general public.

He explained, "When you started crying, everyone in the audience was crying, too. They understood everything you had to say and you did it without making anyone feel bad. That was great, Mom. Thanks for standing up for us."

It was the first time in my life that my son said he was proud of me. I have uttered those words many times to him, but in reverse, it was fantastic to hear, particularly after self condemnation for crying before the general public.

As we walked to the car, I remembered his response when I informed him that I was going to the school board meeting. He said, "Oh, yeah! The counselors at my school were asking me if you would come." He finished with, "I am coming with you." I reminded him that the decision would not affect him because he was graduating. With righteous indignation he replied, "So, these are my friends, my coaches, my teammates. It will affect them. If I can help, I want to be there." I was proud of him and agreed to allow him to come.

Then I uttered, "I am proud of you too, Son. You stood up for what was right in your eyes to help others, without expectation of personal gain. That is the making of a great man. Continue to think that way and God will advance you toward the greater good."

Interestingly enough, the tragedy at the School Board Meeting resulted in a win for my family. I shared a moment with my son that I will never forget. The school system was at the crux of our encounter; yet, it sparked the beginning of an unshakeable realization that the answer to the school systems ills involved community. Parents, students, teachers, principals, counselors, social service agencies, community and clergy were all necessary to fix this broken system. It would truly take a village to solve our problems.

The irony in the meeting was that the school board had no knowledge of my recent tenure as a high school student. They had no knowledge of my experiences. As I had been before my journey in high school, they were at that moment, too far from the educational process to know what its real issues were. They too embraced the perception I had when I embarked upon the experience in high school. We saw school as only students, teachers, text books and little more. However, there is so much more that makes the experience meaningful and they were about to wipe away an entire foundational layer.

One cannot fail to mention the hope that high school coaches provide for students, not only teaching them the social benefits of team work, but opening doors for college scholarship for reasons other than academics. Every student will not be a 4.9 student. Many have other talents and skills that open the doors to higher education. They deserve the opportunity that extra-curricular activities provide.

The library has always been a haven for students to finish homework, to do research, and to study together. It is also a place of safety for students who cannot find safety at home (*These children do exist.*). While unintended, the library serves as a safe and supervised place of waiting for students whose parents' schedules differ from the end of the school day.

The library is the most cost-effective journey to worlds and countries that our children have not seen. For the writer-in-waiting, it is home. And yet, the school board, elected to protect the integrity of the educational process, is preparing to wipe these necessary elements away.

This particular school system has attached the community libraries to the school themselves. Therefore, their students have the benefits of both places in one location. This was great planning ahead; however, a school board without understanding was preparing to permanently alter great planning in a less-than-great way.

With great Purpose comes Great Responsibility

It is unimaginable to envision myself undertaking this writing challenge during my high school years, and yet it was the foundation of a good high school education that paved the way to this opportunity. In recollection, I could not say that any of my teachers or professors would have pegged me as a future writer of America and yet, I am a writer. This realization strongly supports my assertion that purpose is *not* given to man to choose, but granted to him to fulfill. *Teach Because I Came* exposes the gaps in our educational system and proposes a tremendous educational plan designed to close those gaps and meet the needs of all our students.

Teach Because I Came calls for a unification of parents and guardians, school systems, social services, churches, communities and government to assist in this great responsibility to educate our children. With the singular goal of developing productive citizens for our society, its content aims at what is true of mankind. We are not simply physical bodies on this planet. We are equipped with a mind that is phenomenally powerful. Beyond the acceptance of these two facts about humankind is yet another revealing truth that the educational system cannot ignore. Each of us has a soul. It is the part of every human being which makes us the unique bearer of what is necessary to fulfill purpose. Our system of education must recognize, honor, and work to develop the whole child.

Works Consulted

"Action for Healthy Kids: Fact Sheet." April 2012. <http://sboh.wa.gov/Meetings/2003/10_15/documents/pmTab08-Factsheet.pdf>.

Alabama Coalition Against Domestic Violence. "Affects of Domestic Violence on Children." March 2012. <http://www.acadv.org/children.html>.

American Family Physician-Medicine and Society. *"Witnessing Domestic Violence: The Effect on Children."* July 2012. <http://www.aafp.org/afp/2002/1201/p2052.html>.

American Foundation for Suicide Prevention. "Facts and Figures – Suicide". February 2012. <http://www.afsp.org/index.cfm?page_id=04ea1254-bd31-1fa3->

American Heart Association, American Stroke Association. "Statistical Fact Sheet 2012– Update Overweight and Obesity." February 2012. <http://www.heart.org/idc/groups/heart-public/@wcm/@sop/@smd/documents/downloadable/ucm_319588.pdf>

American Psychological Association. "Child Sexual Abuse: What Parents Should Know." September 2012.

<http://www.apa.org/pi/families/resources/child-sexual -abuse.aspx>

Berg, Kris. *Justifying Physical Education Based on Neuroscience Evidence*, JOPERD. March 2010. <http://www.aahperd.org/publications/journals/joperd/justifying-physical-education-based-on-neuroscience-evidence.cfm>

Center for Disease Control and Prevention (CDC). "Attention-Deficit/ Hyperactivity Disorder." April 2013. <http://www.cdc.gov/ncbddd/adhd/data.html>

Center for Disease Control and Prevention (CDC). "Sexual Risk Behavior: HIV, STD & Teen Pregnancy Prevention." July 2012. <www.cdc.gov/HealthyYouth/sexualbehaviors>

Centers for Disease Control and Prevention (CDC). "Youth Risk Behavior Surveillance – United States 2009: Surveillance Summaries-Volume 59/SS-5." March 2012. <http://www.cdc.gov/healthyyouth/yrbs/>

"Child and Adolescent Mental Illness and Drug Abuse Statistics." May 2012. <http://www.aacap.org/cs/root/resources_for_families/child_and_adolescent_mental_illnessstatistics>

Childhelp. "National Child Abuse Statistics." September

2012.
<http//www.childhelp.org/pages/statistics?gclid=CI
6GodCdrLICFQW>.

Child Welfare Information Gateway. April 2012.
<http://www.childwelfare.gov/pubs/factsheets/dome
sticviolence.dfm>.

Child Welfare. "How Parental Substance Use Disorders
Affect Children, Chapter 3." April 2012.
<http://www.childwelfare.gov/pubs/usermanuals/su
bstanceuse/chapterthree.cfm>.

Fagan, Patrick, PhD, World Congress of Families II:
"The Effect of Divorce of Children." November
1999.
<http://www.worldcongress.org/wcf2_spkrs/wcf2_f
agan.htm >.

Gasbarra, Paul. Public Agenda: "Our Money, Our
Schools: Top Ten Findings From our Research
Team." August 2012.
<www.publicagenda.org/print/16983>.

Jeltsen, Melissa. "Bringing Back Home Economics."
May 2012.
<http://childrenshospitalblog.org/bringing-back-
home-economics/>

National Alliance on Mental Illness (NAMI): "Mental
Illness: Facts and Numbers." September 2012.
<http://www.nami.org/Template.cfm?Section=Abo

ut_Mental_Illness&Template=/ContentManagemen
t/ContentDisplay.cfm&ContentID=53155>.

National Association for Children of Alcoholics
(NACA): "Children of Addicted Parents: Important
Facts."   February   2012.
<http://www.nacoa.net/pdfs/addicted/pdf/>.

National Association for the Education of Homeless
Children and Youth: "Facts about Homeless
Education."   July   2012.
<http://www.naehcy.org.fact.html>.

National Center for Children Exposed to Violence.
March 2012.
<http://www.nccev.org/violence/domestic.html>.

National Coalition for the Homeless, Washington, D.C:
"Education of Homeless Youth and Children."
September   2009.
<www.nationalhomeless.org/factsheets/education.h
tml>.

National Survey of Children's Health-2007. "Time Spent
Watching TV or Playing Video Games." September
2012.
<http://childhealthdata.org/browse/survey/resultls?
q=283&r+1>.

National Vital Statistics System. "National Marriage and
Divorce   Rate   Trends."   March   2013.
<http://www.cdc.gov/nchs/nvss/marriage_divorce_t
ables.htm>.

Office of National Drug Control Policy-Executive Office of the President. "Fact Sheet: Consequences of Illicit Drug Use in America." March 2012. <www.whitehouse.gov/sites/default/files/ondcp/2012_ndcs.pd>.

Oskin, Becky. Fox News. "Teen and Video Games: How Much is too Much?" August 13, 2012. (Reviewed: September 21, 2012). <http://www.foxnews.com/health/2012/08/13/teens-and-video-games-how-much-is-too-much/#ixzz278sTlOHn>.

Prison Fellowship:DeMossNews.com. "Statistics Concerning Children of Prisoners." April 2012. <http://www.demossnewspond.com/pf/additional/statistics_concerning_children_of_prisoners>.

Rand Corporation: "Effects of Soldiers Deployment on Children's Academic Performance and Behavioral Health." September 2012. <http://www.rand.org/content/dam/rand/pubs/monographs/2011/RAND_MG1095.pdf >.

Richtel, Matt. "Growing Up Digital, Wired for Distraction." The New York Times Newspaper. November 21, 2010. <www.nytimes.com/2010/11/21/technology/21brain.html?pagewanted>.

U.S. Department of Health & Human Services –

Administration for Children and Families, Administration on Children, Youth and Families, Children's Bureau Maltreatment Types. "Child Maltreatment Data Tables 2010-21st Year of Reporting." Table 2-4. http://www.acf.hhs.gov/programs/cb/pubs/cm10/cm10.pdf.

Video Game Statistics Industry Figures and Information. "Video Game Industry Stats," September 2012, <http://www.grabstats.com/statcategorymainaspc?statCatID=13>.

Waugh, Rob. Daily Mail. co.uk. "Violent Games Do Alter Your Brain," Sept. 2012. <http://www.dailymail.co.uk/sciencetech/article-2067607/Violent-games-DO-alter-brain--effect-visible-MRI-scans-just-week.html#ixzz2797eHRqY>.

About the Author

Michele Owes, author of *Pearls of Wisdom for Our Daughters*, is a graduate of Kent State University who has extensive experience in the field of education as a principal, administrator, teacher, corporate trainer, and curriculum writer. As a certified neurofeedback specialist, she has worked to assist children, providing a non-drug, non-invasive solution to learning difficulties, including ADD and ADHD. *Teach Because I Came* is a culmination of her experiences and an opportunity to journey with her as she shadows a senior in one of America's high schools. You will laugh and cry as she reveals the contents of her heart and unfolds a Comprehensive Educational Plan. Every educator, administrator, student and School Board *needs* a copy of this book. It will change you.

Michele Owes enjoys her life with her husband Joseph, who is also her Pastor. They have four amazing children. She is grateful for the experiences that God has afforded her family which ultimately gives substance to her writing. She is thankful that necessity was laid at her feet and God's grace allowed her to respond to the call.

Made in the USA
Middletown, DE
16 October 2022

12887357R00129